MEDIA ARABIC

ISLAMIC SURVEYS SERIES

MEDIA ARABIC

JULIA ASHTIANY

EDINBURGH UNIVERSITY PRESS

© Julia Ashtiany, 1993

Edinburgh University Press Ltd
22 George Square, Edinburgh

Typset in Linotron Ehrhardt
by Koinonia Ltd, Bury, and
printed and bound in Great Britain
by Short Run Press Ltd, Exeter

A CIP record for this book is
available from the British Library

ISBN 0 7486 0367 0

From news and current affairs to pop
music and cultural programmes, the
BBC's Arabic Service broadcasts for
$10\frac{1}{2}$ hours a day to the Arab world,
the extracts on the cassette produced
to accompany this book being read by
native speakers from a range of Arab
countries.

$22.72 Blackwell 11-24-93 (80)

Contents

Part II

Acknowledgements

I wish to thank first and foremost Professor J. D. Latham, Professor of Arabic and Islamic Studies at the University of Edinburgh until 1988, who first suggested this course in Media Arabic, for his continuing support and kindness. I am also grateful to my former students and colleagues at the University of Edinburgh, particularly Dr Carole Hillenbrand, Reader in Arabic and Islamic Studies, who encouraged me to publish, and to Edinburgh University Press, and to Ivor Normand and Brigit Viney, editors, for their patience during the processes of rewriting and production.

It is a great pleasure to record my thanks to the following, for their help in obtaining material: David Buckley, Deputy Head, BBC Arabic Service; Brad Hansen, US State Department; Ayaz Taj Al-Garabeh; and the editors of Al-Ahram International, Asharq Al-Awsat and Al-Hayat for permission to quote and reproduce material. I also wish to thank Dr Eugene Rogan, St Antony's College Middle East Centre, Oxford, and Hassan Abuala, Ali Assad, Amal Hindawi and Nada El-Muhtadi, newsreaders at the BBC Arabic Service, for their help in recording the tape which accompanies this book.

Introduction

There is a growing demand among students of Arabic for access to the Arab media, which often cover stories not reported fully in the western media. The language of the Arab press and radio also has features which make it especially suitable as a basis for learning wider skills of communication.

This book is an expanded version of a course designed for and taught in the Department of Islamic and Middle Eastern Studies at the University of Edinburgh from 1988 to 1991. It provides intermediate-level students with an introduction to the language of the Arab media and develops their basic listening and interpreting skills.

'Media Arabic' is here taken to mean the language of ordinary news items, printed or broadcast. Such items have a limited stylistic and syntactic range, which arguably makes Media Arabic unsuitable for use as a general introduction to contemporary Arabic. This same limitation, however, makes Media Arabic an excellent medium for all forms of aural/oral work. The course is aimed at students who have mastered basic grammar, acquired a small vocabulary, and will be able to some degree to appreciate the stylistic and other differences between Media Arabic and Modern Standard Arabic. It is intended as a supplement to language-teaching based on Modern Standard Arabic.

Part I provides an introduction to the structures and formats of Media Arabic which most obviously differ from those of Modern Standard Arabic and which initially form the greatest barrier to comprehension. Recognition and manipulation of typical Media Arabic structures is learned through a combination of oral/aural and reading exercises. Part I can be used on its own by students who merely wish to learn to read the newspapers, while Part II lays greater emphasis on aural comprehension and basic interpreting.

Bearing in mind the need for flexibility, Part I has been designed for use in classes of varying sizes and with students of either a basic or a more advanced level of fluency. Exercises marked with an asterisk are for more advanced students; they may also be used as supplementary material or in more intensive teaching. It is assumed that a uniform level of fluency will have been achieved by the end of Part I. In Part II, asterisks mark a series of optional homework exercises, which use taped material from the BBC Arabic Service.

HOW TO USE THIS COURSE

This book is not intended as a comprehensive guide to the Arab press and broadcast media, and does not attempt to evaluate their role or content; it is a language course, and confines itself to the more basic forms of Arabic journalese.

It is designed primarily for use in the classroom, not for self-teaching, and, for best results, it is recommended that it be taught in two-hour sessions. My experience suggests that students find it hard to warm up in shorter sessions, and that full concentration and fluency are only reached in the second hour. Each lesson should, in theory, take one, or at most two, two-hour sessions to complete. In practice, however, teachers may find that any given group of students seldom maintains an absolutely consistent rate of learning, and that it is better to vary the pace accordingly than to insist that each lesson be completed within a prescribed limit.

The bulk of the text consists of examples and exercises. Explanations are generally brief, and are confined to features characteristic of Media Arabic. There are no explanations of general points of Modern Standard Arabic grammar. The need for such explanations will vary depending on the general course of study being followed by any given group of students, and individual teachers will know best what their group requires in terms of supplementary information.

The explanations highlight for both teacher and students the main points illustrated in the examples. Teachers may, however, prefer to direct students' attention straight to the examples, and to explain these points in their own way, together with any points of Modern Standard Arabic grammar that may arise. The explanations in the text may then be used by students as an aid to revision .

Explanations take the following form. Each unit is prefaced by 'General Remarks' which describe briefly the general features of the Arabic material to be introduced, and the particular skills which the exercises are designed to develop. Each lesson within the unit then has a heading or series of headings describing the type of vocabulary that it contains. (Occasional footnotes explain miscellaneous points of structure or translation.) The primary emphasis is thus on skills, and not on the acquisition of vocabulary as such. To clarify this point: basic Media Arabic, like other basic forms of journalese, consists largely of clichés which occur in predictable structural and semantic slots. To learn one word or phrase, therefore, is to be introduced to a family of words or phrases of similar meaning and function (e.g. verbs or phrases introducing statements and reports: 'the prime minister has said'; 'the minister announced'; 'our correspondent reports'; 'our correspondent reports that the prime minister has said that the education minister will announce', etc.). The learner who has identified the function of such items is on the way to developing the skills of using them in appropriate contexts and of making a reasonable guess at the meaning of phrases occurring in similar slots.

This approach might seem over-mechanistic; but I have found that what encourages an inflexible approach to language learning is, on the contrary, the widely-accepted practice of appending ready-made vocabulary lists to sections of text and making these the focus of learning. I have provided no vocabulary lists, and have generally avoided giving 'model' translations of examples, in order to emphasise that the meaning (and appropriate use and translation) of many words is determined by context. This practice also has the advantage of obliging students to learn vocabulary progressively. If they have failed to learn the vocabulary in one lesson, having no crib to fall back on, they cannot move on to the next. (It will, however, be observed that, in every lesson in Part I, nearly all the vocabulary used in the Arabic text is mirrored in the English text, and vice versa.)

It is hoped that this approach will encourage students to assess their own progress in terms of what they have learned to do, rather than in terms of the number of new words encountered. A little vocabulary can be made to go a long way with the appropriate skills; the goal of this course is to encourage the learner to develop a small but always active vocabulary (as opposed to the extensive but largely passive vocabulary acquired through the reading of literary texts).

Finally, the exercises have been devised so as to emphasise as much as possible the difference between classroom work and home study. The resources of the classroom (the presence of the teacher, the opportunities for group and oral work) cannot be duplicated in the study; conversely, home study develops disciplines of learning and self-teaching skills which cannot be acquired in a group. In Part I, homework exercises are designed to help students to revise and develop a regular habit of consolidating learning begun in the classroom; no new material is introduced except in the asterisked items. In Part II, homework exercises include preparation as well as revision. They are designed as a structured introduction to independent reading, and show some of the ways in which the media can be used systematically as a source of linguistic information. The optional taped homework material accompanying Units 7–10 is graduated and loosely related to previously reviewed material, but is otherwise unstructured, and provides opportunities for fully independent linguistic work.

It is recommended that teachers avoid spending classroom time on reviewing written work. Any written work done in the classroom should be marked and returned with the previous session's homework. Exceptions to this are dictations, which can be quickly assessed in the classroom by both teacher and students, and other classroom exercises where the instructions specifically state that students should compare their copy with the printed text or read their work aloud.

It should finally be noted that *all Oral Exercises, whether Arabic–English or English–Arabic, are closed book exercises*, that is to say, the text is to be read out by the teacher to the students for oral translation, and students should not consult the text during this process.

THE MATERIAL

The material used dates from late 1989 to early 1992 for the most part. The international editions of the large-circulation dailies are the main source, with some examples being taken from the local presses of North Africa, Yemen and the Gulf.

Characteristic departures from correct Modern Standard Arabic grammar have not been amended, and are indicated in notes. Short vowels have occasionally been added as an aid to learning. Initial *hamzah* has been added only sporadically, following newspaper usage. Note that where current pronunciations diverge from the vowelling given in dictionaries – for example, *falasṭīnī* for *filasṭīnī*, *dawlī* for both *dawlī* and *duwalī* – no vowelling has been indicated. Vowelling is also omitted in the case of words with received variants, for example, *yashmulu/yashmilu*, *'unf/ 'anf*.

Similarly, in the case of the taped material which accompanies Units 7–10 as optional homework material, the prime consideration has been authenticity rather than textbook standards of correctness. The pressures of preparing news for broadcasting and of broadcasting live give rise to some special features, such as improvised and ephemeral coinages and the occasional misreading or mispronunciation. It is these features which present the new listener with the greatest problems of comprehension, and I think it essential that the learner should be progressively introduced to them. The news items accompanying Units 7–9 have been selected from a number of BBC Arabic Service news broadcasts dating from 1989 to 1992, and have been specially re-recorded by Arabic Service newsreaders for this course; the complete Arabic Service news bulletin which accompanies Unit 10 was taped live. The BBC 's Arabic Service is widely listened to in the Middle East, and Arab journalists acknowledge the formative influence that it continues to exercise on broadcasting formats and on Media Arabic generally. Like the majority of printed sources in this book, the items chosen illustrate the international version (and pronunciation) of Media Arabic rather than its local variants.

The question of the local variations – in choices of vocabulary and forms of presentation, etc. – which exist in Media Arabic, whether written or broadcast, raises a wider issue. Media Arabic is an increasingly challenging field. Even in the comparatively unified area of international Arabic journalism, style and vocabulary are continually evolving, and as the world picture continues to change in unforeseen ways, it becomes difficult to decide which topics to select as the main focus of study. In any event, it would be misleading to suggest that a course such as this can provide students with a standard or comprehensive vocabulary which will need no significant revision in subsequent phases of their careers. In addition, the more sophisticated levels of journalism, such as editorials, lie outside its scope (a few examples are given, simply as illustrations, in Unit 5). This book is no more than an introduction to the basic language of the media, but one which I hope will help to equip the learner for independent study.

Key to Transliteration

The system of transliteration followed is that prescribed by the Encyclo-paedia of Islam, with *j* instead of *dj* and *q* instead of *k*̣; *tā' marbūṭah* is rendered as *-ah* (*-at* in *iḍāfah*). Newspaper titles are transliterated following this system (except in the Acknowledgements, where the English forms used by the newspapers themselves are given). Arabic names have not been transliterated where familiar English forms exist (for example, King Hussein, not King Ḥusayn; Yasser Arafat, not Yāsir ʿArafāt; Baʾath Party, not Baʿth Party).

Key to Symbols

In Part I, an asterisk preceding an exercise heading denotes advanced or supplementary material. In Part II, asterisks mark a different series of optional homework exercises, which use taped material from the BBC Arabic Service.

Part I

UNIT I

Preparatory Exercises

'Media Arabic', for the purposes of this course, means the Arabic of the daily press and of broadcast news. The bulk of the material studied consists of simple news items.

Two kinds of exercise are given special emphasis: aural comprehension, and oral translation both into and out of Arabic.

News broadcasts, on which the comprehension exercises are partly modelled, are often delivered at high speed, sometimes with full grammatical vowelling; oral translation demands the ability to produce basic word and sentence forms accurately and confidently. A good grasp of basic grammar is therefore desirable from the start. In the initial stages of learning, particular attention should be paid to word forms, including: plurals of nouns; the passive of verbs; the dual; numbers. The exercises in Unit I provide some opportunities for revising these points.

The basic vocabulary and syntax of Media Arabic are the same as those of Modern Standard Arabic. However, like English journalese, Media Arabic is also a language within a language, favouring certain constructions and items of vocabulary. Such stereotyped items can be learned by rote. As one of the chief difficulties of media Arabic lies in manipulating its generally rigid structures when translating at speed, it is advisable always to learn items of vocabulary together with the phrases in which they most often occur, that is, as small structural units rather than as isolated items. The exercises which follow each lesson are designed to encourage this practice.

LESSON I.I: REPORTS AND STATEMENTS

Very many news reports deal with statements made by or about public
figures. In order to vary the texture of such news items, Media Arabic
uses numerous synonyms and near-synonyms of the verb *qāla*, 'to say'.
These verbs should be translated according to context and in accordance
with English journalistic style rather than strictly according to the
dictionary. Each verb has its own characteristic construction, which must
be learned as part of the verb.

Below are examples of how some of the most common of these verbs
are used. A general sense is given for each verb. Study the examples and
find your own translations of the verbs according to context.

> Note that, as well as the underlined words, the main items of
> vocabulary illustrated in these and subsequent examples will be
> used again in the exercises.

Examples

'to say':

قال

ـ يقول مراسلنا في الجزائر إنَّ الشعبَ يريد الإصلاح .

ـ يقول مراسل هيئة الإذاعة البريطانية في الجزائر إنَّ
الجزائريينَ يريدون الإصلاح .

Near-synonym (general sense: 'to mention'):

ذكر

ـ يذكر مراسل هيئة الإذاعة البريطانية في الجزائر أنَّ الوضْعَ
خطير جدا .

ـ ذكر مراسلنا التطوراتِ الأخيرةَ في البلاد وقال إنّها قد تؤدّي
الى وضْع خطير جدا .

Near-synonym (general sense: 'to assure', 'to confirm'):

أكّد

ـ يؤكّد الوزير أنَّ أغلبية الجزائريين تريد الإصلاح .

ـ أكّد وزير الخارجية البريطاني تقديرَ بلاده لجهودالجزائر مِن أجْلِ
الإصلاح .

Near-synonym (general sense: 'to declare', 'to state'):

صرّح بأنَّ

ـ صرَّحت الصحف الجزائرية **بأنَّ** رئيسَ الوزراء الجزائري سيزور ليبيا في الشهر القادم .

ـ صرَّح الرئيس لـ مراسلنا **بأنَّه** يؤيّد الإصلاح .

Two other frequently-encountered verbs are:

'to express':

أعْرب عن

ـ أُعْرِبت رئيسة الوزراء السابقة **عن** تقديرها لجهود الرئيس الجزائري السابق من أجْل الإصلاح .

'to announce':

أعْلن

ـ أعْلن الرئيس الجزائري بَرْنامَجَ إصلاحات اجتماعية واقتصادية ودُسْتورية .

ـ أعْلن الرئيس أنَّه سيزور الجزائر .

ـ أعلنت الحكومة الهندية الحربَ على الصين .

CLASSROOM PRACTICE

1.1.1 Oral Exercise

Listen to the following sentences, which will be read aloud by the teacher. Translate them orally into English.

١ـ يذكر مراسلنا أن الوضع خطير جدا.

٢ـ يذكر مراسلنا أن الوضع الاقتصادي خطير جدا وأن الشعب يريد الإصلاح.

٣ـ أكد الرئيس أن التطورات الأخيرة قد أدت إلى وضع خطير جدا.

٤ـ يذكر مراسل هيئة الإذاعة البريطانية في الجزائر أن الرئيس الجزائري سيعلن برنامج إصلاحات في المستقبل القريب.

٥ـ يؤكد الرئيس الجزائري أن أغلبية الشعب الجزائري تريد الإصلاح.

٦ـ صرح رئيس الوزراء الفرنسي بأن وزير الخارجية الفرنسي سيزور ليبيا في المستقبل القريب.

٧ـ أعربت رئيسة الوزراء الفرنسية السابقة عن تقديرها لجهود الرئيس الجزائري السابق من أجل الإصلاح الدستوري.

٨ـ صرح وزير الخارجية الفرنسي بأن رئيس الوزراء الفرنسي سيزور الجزائر في الشهر القادم ليعرب عن تقديره لجهود الرئيس الجزائري من أجل الإصلاح الاقتصادي.

٩ـ يُذكر في الجزائر أن الرئيس قد يعلن برنامجا اقتصاديا جديدا في المستقبل القريب.

١٠ـ صرح الرئيس لمراسل هيئة الإذاعة البريطانية بأن الشعب يريد السلام وأعرب عن تأييده لجهود الرئيس الأمريكي من أجل السلام في الشرق الأوسط.

*1.1.2 Oral Exercise

Listen to the following sentences, which will be read aloud by the teacher. Translate them orally into English.

١ـ أعلن الرئيس الجزائري أنه سيزور ليبيا في المستقبل القريب.

٢ـ ذكر الرئيس التطورات الأخيرة في بلاده وأكد تقديره لجهود رئيس الوزراء من أجل الإصلاح.

٣ـ أكد الرئيس أن بلاده لا تريد الحرب وأنها لن تعلن الحرب.

٤ـ أُعلن في باريس أمس أن الرئيس الجزائري الجديد سيزور فرنسا في الشهر القادم.

٥ـ أُعلنت برامج إصلاحات مختلفة في الجزائر أمس.

٦ـ يُذكر أن الوضع السياسي في البلاد قد أصبح خطيرا جدا.

٧ـ تقول الصحف الجزائرية إن الجزائريين يريدون الإصلاح الاقتصادي أكثر منهم يريدون الإصلاح الدستوري.

٨ـ صرحت الحكومة البريطانية بأنها تؤيد جهود الرئيس الأمريكي من أجل السلام في الشرق الأوسط.

٩ـ أكد الرئيس الجزائري تأييده لجهود الرئيس الأمريكي.

١٠ـ أعرب الرئيس الأمريكي عن تقديره لجهود الرؤساء العرب من أجل السلام في الشرق الأوسط.

1.1.3 Written Exercise

1. Listen to the following passage, which will be read aloud twice at dictation speed by the teacher. As you listen, write an English translation of the passage.
2. Listen to the same passage being read aloud again, and write it down in Arabic. Compare your version with the text below.

يقول مراسل هيئة الإذاعة البريطانية في الجزائر إن أغلبية الجزائريين تريد الإصلاح ، ويذكر أن الرئيس الجزائري الجديد سوف يعلن برنامج إصلاحات اجتماعية واقتصادية ودستورية. ويقول مراسلنا إن رئيس الوزراء الجزائري قد أعرب عن تقدير البرلمان الجزائري لجهود الرئيس السابق من أجل الإصلاح.

1.1.4 Oral Exercise

Translate the following sentences into Arabic:

1. The British Foreign Secretary has announced that he is to visit Algeria.
2. Our correspondent in London says that the Foreign Secretary will be going to Algeria next month.
3. The BBC correspondent in Paris says that the French Foreign Minister may visit Algiers† in the near future.
4. The minister says that the majority of Algerians want reform.

†When the names of a country and its capital are identical, the capital may be distinguished by putting *al-'aṣimah* in apposition to it: *al-jazā'ir al-'aṣimah* = Algiers.

5. She expressed her appreciation of the President's efforts to promote reform.
6. Our correspondent reports that the situation has become serious and could lead to war.
7. The Algerian papers say that the economic situation could become very serious.
8. Our correspondent says that the situation is grave, but that the majority of the people want reform, not war.
9. China may declare war on India.
10. The minister affirmed that his country did not want war.

*1.1.5 Oral Exercise

Translate the following sentences into Arabic:

1. It is reported in Algiers that the president may go to Paris next month.
2. The president is shortly to announce a new economic programme.
3. It has been announced in London that the Foreign Secretary will not be going to Brussels next month.
4. The Iraqi press reports that the president has declared that the Iraqi people do not want constitutional reform.
5. She referred to recent developments in her country, and said that the political situation was now very serious.
6. Next month, the president is to announce a programme of social, economic and constitutional reforms.
7. A new economic programme was announced in Algiers yesterday.
8. The BBC correspondent in Algiers says that a new economic programme is to be announced in the near future.
9. Our correspondent says that a new economic programme is to be announced by the president next week.
10. The Foreign Minister confirmed that the latest political developments in his country could lead to war.

1.1.6 Written Exercise

Listen to sentences from 1.1.4 Oral Exercise being read aloud at dictation speed by the teacher. As you listen, write an Arabic translation of the sentences.

*1.1.7 Written Exercise

Listen to sentences from 1.1.5 Oral Exercise being read aloud at dictation speed by the teacher. As you listen, write an Arabic translation of the sentences.

HOMEWORK

1. Written translation of 1.1.1 Oral Exercise.
*2. Written translation of 1.1.2 Oral Exercise.
3. Written translation of 1.1.4 Oral Exercise.
*4. Written translation of 1.1.5 Oral Exercise.
5. Use each of the following words/phrases in a complete Arabic sentence of your own:

أَيَّدَ ـ أَدَّى إلى ـ أَكَّدَ ـ مِن أَجْلِ ... ـ سابِقٌ

REVISION

1.1.8 Oral Exercise

Listen to the first eight sentences following, which will be read aloud by the teacher. Translate them orally into English. Then read numbers 9 and 10 aloud and translate them orally into English.

١ـ لا شكٌ في أنَّ شعوب أوروبا الشرقية تريد † الإصلاح.

٢ـ يبدو أنَّ أغلبية شعوب أوروبا الشرقية يريدون † الإصلاح.

٣ـ يقول مراسلنا في لندن ان رئيس الوزراء البريطاني سيزور المملكة العربية السعودية في المستقبل القريب.

٤ـ يقول مراسل هيئة الإذاعة البريطانية في الرياض ان رئيسة الوزراء البريطانية السابقة ستزور السعودية في المستقبل القريب.

٥ـ أعرب رئيس الوزراء السابق عن تقديره لجهود الرئيس السوفياتي من أجل الإصلاح.

٦ـ أعرب الرئيس المصري عن تقديره لجهود الرئيس الأمريكي من أجل السلام في الشرق الأوسط.

---

†Note the alternation between grammatical and logical agreement.

٧ـ أكد وزير الدولة البريطاني للشؤون الخارجية تقدير بلاده لجهود الرئيس المصري حُسْني مُبارَك من أجل السلام في الشرق الأوسط.

٨ـ أكد الرئيس الأمريكي بيل كلينتون انه يؤيد جهود الرئيس المصري حسني مبارك من أجل السلام.

٩ـ إذاعات مصر المسموعة في الخارج

البرنامج العامّ

نَشْرَة الأخبار	١٤،...
آخِر الأنباء	٢٣،...

صوت العرب

النشرة الأخبارية الأولى	١،٣٠
النشرة الأخبارية الثانية	٨،...
مُوجَز الأنباء	١٣،...

١٠ـ يُذاع البرنامج يومَ الأربعاء وتُعاد إذاعته يومَ الخميس.

1.1.9 Oral Exercise

Listen to the first eight sentences following, which will be read aloud by
the teacher. Translate them orally into English. Then read numbers 9 and
10 aloud and translate them orally into English.

١ـ ذكر الرئيس السوفياتي السابق التطورات الأخيرة في بلاده
وأكد انه يؤيد الإصلاح.

٢ـ أكدت رئيسة الوزراء السابقة انها تؤيد الحكومة وقالت لا شكَّ
في أنَّ أغلبية الشعب البريطاني تؤيد برنامج الحكومة الاقتصادي.

٣ـ قد تعلن الحكومة برنامجها الاقتصادي الجديد في المستقبل
القريب.

٤ـ تذكر الصحف البريطانية ان رئيس الوزراء البريطاني قد لا
يزور بروكسل الأسبوع القادم.

٥ـ صرح الرئيس الجديد لمراسلنا بأن الدستور يحتاج الى إصلاح.

٦ـ صرح الرئيس المصري لمراسل هيئة الإذاعة البريطانية في
القاهرة بأن الشعب المصري يريد السلام في الشرق الاوسط.

٧ـ صرح رئيس الوزراء للصحف بأن حكومته قد تحتاج الى
تأييد رئيس الوزراء السابق في المستقبل القريب.

٨ـ قال رئيس الوزراء ان الدستور لا بُدَّ من إصلاحه في
المستقبل القريب.

٩ـ تلفزيون لبنان
البرنامج الأول

١٢،٠٠ موسيقى ـ ١٢،٣٠ صور متحرّكة ـ ١،٠٠ أُغنيات
أجنبية على طلب المشاهدين ـ ٤،٠٠ فيلم أميركي ـ ٦،٣٠
برنامج للأطفال ـ ٧،٣٠ الأخبار ـ ٨،٠٠ فيلم أجنبي

١. القسم العربي بهيئة الاذاعة البريطانية

مختارات من برامجنا

"العالم هذا المساء" يذاع في الساعة ٦.١٥ مساء كل أيام الأسبوع . "حديث شؤون الساعة" يذاع الساعة ٥.٠٢ مساء من الاثنين الى الجمعة وتعاد إذاعته في يومه الساعة ٧.٠٢ مساء.

*1.1.10 *Written Exercise*

Listen to sentences from 1.1.8 Oral Exercise and/or 1.1.9 Oral Exercise being read aloud at dictation speed by the teacher. As you listen, write an English translation of the sentences.

1.1.11 Oral Exercise

Translate the following sentences into Arabic:

1. The British press reports that the ex-prime minister is to visit Poland.
2. The newspapers say that the political situation is grave and that recent developments could lead to war.
3. The Russian newspapers say that the former Soviet president has announced that he will be visiting Saudi Arabia in the near future.
4. The BBC's Warsaw correspondent reports that it has been announced that the former Soviet president is to visit the Polish capital in the course of the coming weeks.
5. According to the BBC's Washington correspondent, it has been announced that the former Soviet president is to visit the USA shortly to express his appreciation of the American people's support for him.
6. The president has told our correspondent that his people do not want war.
7. The former prime minister affirmed her support for the government.
8. There are reports that the former prime minister may not lend her support to the government's economic programme.
9. The American president is said to support Egypt's economic reform programme.
10. The prime minister told our correspondent that the situation was grave, and remarked that his country might need America's support in the near future.

1.1.12 Oral Exercise

Translate the following sentences into Arabic:

1. Our correspondent in Russia reports that the economic situation is graver than last year.
2. The president told British newspaper correspondents that reform was inevitable.
3. The prime minister has told reporters that the British government may not support a European economic programme.
4. Referring to a programme broadcast last week, the prime minister told reporters that his government could do without the ex-prime minister's support.
5. The Foreign Secretary has confirmed that he will not be going to Brussels next week.
6. The president declared that the Polish people needed social and economic reform, not a new constitution.
7. The majority of Arab heads of state support the American peace effort.
8. Egypt's President Mubarak has told President Clinton that the majority of Arab leaders support the American peace effort in the Middle East.
9. According to our Middle East correspondent the Egyptian Foreign Minister told Israeli reporters that most Arab and European leaders support America's Middle East peace effort.
10. It was announced in Riyadh that the Saudi Foreign Minister would not be going to Washington.

1.1.13 Written Exercise

Listen to sentences from 1.1.11 Oral Exercise and/or 1.1.12 Oral Exercise being read aloud at dictation speed by the teacher. As you listen, write an Arabic translation of the sentences.

LESSON 1.2: VISITS

A large number of news items deal with the visits, messages and meetings of public figures. Such items can form the bulk of broadcast news in, for example, Saudi Arabia. Their information content varies; some provide pointers to political and commercial developments not normally covered in the British daily press.

Below are examples of some of the commonest expressions used in connection with visits. Study the examples and translate them orally before doing the classroom exercises.

Examples

ـ يذكر مراسلنا في الخليج ان نائب وزير الخارجية الإيراني يزور مَسْقَط حاليا.

ـ قد وصل نائب وزير الخارجية الإيراني مسقط أمس.

ـ زعيم المُعارَضَة السودانية يصل إلى القاهرة غدا.

Note the two constructions of *waṣala*.
Note that the word order of the third example is that of a headline.

ـ يصل إلى القاهرة غدا زعيم المعارضة السودانية في زيارة رسمية.

ـ وصل الرئيس الفرنسي الدار البيضاء في زيارة خاصّة.

ـ وصل الرئيس الفرنسي الدار البيضاء في زيارة خاصّة لـ المغرب تستغرق يومين.

ـ وزير خارجية إسبانيا يؤجّل زيارته إلى المغرب.

> Note the two constructions of *ziyārah*.

ـ أمير قَطَر يبدأ زيارةً رسميّة لـ مصر بِدَعوَةٍ من الرئيس مبارك .

ـ وزير صيني يختتم زيارته لـ إمارات .

ـ غادرَ وزير العلاقات الاقتصادية والتجارة الخارجية الصيني الشارْقة صباح أمس في خِتام زيارته لـ دولة الإمارات المتحدة.

ـ قد اجتمع الوزير الصيني قبل المُغادرة مع حاكم الشارْقة، وسيجتمع في طريق عَوْدَته من الإمارات مع الرئيس الهندي.

CLASSROOM PRACTICE

1.2.1 Written Exercise

1. Listen to the following passage, which will be read aloud twice at dictation speed by the teacher. As you listen, write an English translation of the passage.

سيصل نائب وزير الخارجية الجزائري الى القاهرة غدا في زيارة رسمية تستغرق يومين . ويذكر مراسل هيئة الاذاعة البريطانية في الشرق الاوسط ان نائب وزير الخارجية الجزائري يزور مِنْطَقة الخليج حاليا وانه قد أجّل زيارته الى مصر مرّتين .

2. Listen to the same passage being read aloud again, and write it down in Arabic. Compare your version with the text above.

1.2.2 Oral Exercise

Translate the following sentences into Arabic:

1. The Chinese Foreign Trade Minister arrived in Paris yesterday on an official visit.
2. The leader of the Sudanese opposition arrived in Libya this morning on a two-hour visit.
3. The leader of the Sudanese opposition left Libya yesterday at the end of a three-day private visit.

4. The French Foreign Minister is to go to Cairo next month on a two-day official visit at the invitation of President Mubarak.
5. The British Foreign Secretary and the French prime minister will be going to Brussels next month.
6. It is reported from Baghdad that two Yemeni ministers ended a three-day stay in the Iraqi capital yesterday.
7. It is reported in Riyadh that the British Foreign Secretary and the French Minister of Trade are to pay a one-week visit to the Saudi capital during the coming week, at the invitation of the Saudi Ministry of Trade.
8. Lady Thatcher ends private US visit.
9. Foreign Secretary postpones Gulf visit but says 'Gulf states know that Britain backs them'.
10. Ex-president Reagan is on his way back to the United States after a week-long private visit to London where he called at 10 Downing Street before leaving.

1.2.3 Oral Exercise

Translate the following sentences into Arabic.

1. Eleven European prime ministers arrive in Brussels tomorrow.
2. Thirteen African presidents left Cairo yesterday.
3. All the European prime ministers will be going to Brussels next month.
4. All the Arab leaders will be going to Cairo next week.
5. A hundred Arab correspondents have arrived in Washington.
6. More than 1,000 correspondents will be going to Washington at the invitation of the president.
7. It is reported that more than 2,000 Russian students will be leaving Washington tomorrow, ending a month-long stay in the United States.
8. It is reported that more than 1,000,000 Kurds have already arrived in Iran.
9. Fewer than two-thirds of the Americans who visit Britain this year will come to Scotland.
10. Fewer than half the Britons who visit the Continent each year can speak a European language.

HOMEWORK

1. Compile a list of the Arabic names of cities, countries and regions and adjectives of nationality used in Lessons 1.1 and 1.2.
2. Written translation of 1.2.2 Oral Exercise.
*3. Written translation of 1.2.3 Oral Exercise.
4. Use each of the following words/phrases in a complete Arabic sentence of your own:

تطوّراتٌ ـ حالياً ـ اِجْتَمَعَ مَعَ ـ زَعيمُ المُعارَضَةِ ـ عَلاقاتٌ ـ
أَذَاعَ ـ مِنْطَقَةٌ ـ أَجَّلَ ـ اِخْتَتَمَ

Analysis and Comprehension

News items dealing with visits (Unit 1, Lesson 1.2), messages and meetings (this unit, Lesson 2.2) contain numerous official titles. No overall attempt will be made to codify them here, and for general purposes only the most common need be memorised. However, the ability to recognise titles, or to identify a group of words as forming a title, obviously plays a major part in comprehension in the context of foreign affairs. This unit aims to develop the ability to recognise such 'units of comprehension'.

From the point of view of translation and interpretation, note that the circumlocutions *al-'āhil al-urdunnī* (= King Hussein of Jordan), *al-'āhil al-maghribī* (= King Hassan of Morocco), etc. are used chiefly for the sake of variety, while the style *khādim al-ḥaramayn al-sharīfayn* , used by King Fahd of Saudi Arabia, has specific political connotations, since it emphasises the king's guardianship of the Holy Places rather than his status as sovereign .

Note also that the titles of political, administrative and military posts and institutions may vary from country to country in the Arab world and may have no ready-made English counterparts. By contrast, a generally uniform terminology is used for foreign and international institutions, though, as will have been noted in Unit 1, their English translations may vary according to context, for example *wazīr al-khārijiyyah al-isbānī*, 'the Spanish Foreign Minister', but *wazīr al-khārijiyyah al-b(i)rīṭānī*, 'the British Foreign Secretary'.

The word *mas'ūl* may be used to refer to officials and functionaries. The word *shakhṣiyyah* is used of persons whose roles are unspecified. In the examples which occur in the following lessons, consider the advantages that the use of such unspecific terms may offer when translating into Arabic, and the corresponding difficulties that they may pose when translating into English.

LESSON 2.1: TITLES

The following passages contain examples of titles, names of posts or institutions, etc. They also contain additions to the vocabulary of visits, and further expressions of date, time and number. Read them aloud, identify and analyse new terms, and translate orally.

Examples

١ـ وصل وزير الدِّفاع الامريكي المَنامة امس قادما من سلْطنة عُمان.

٢ـ يصل الى القاهرة غدا الجمعة زعيم حزب الشعب الديمقراطي السوداني وزعيم المعارضة في زيارة الى مصر تستغرق عِدَّةُ أيامٍ.

٣ـ غادر مساء امس الاول الرِّباط الرئيس الامريكي السابق رونلد ريجان بعد زيارة خاصة للمغرب استغرقت بِضْعَةُ أيامٍ.

٤ـ وصل عبد الرحيم بو عبيد الأمين العامّ لحزب الاتحاد الاشتراكي للقوّات الشعبية الى المغرب آتيا من فرنسا حيث مضى عدة ايام.

٥ـ وصل الرئيس الفلسطيني ياسر عرفات امس الاربعاء الى الرباط. وتأتي زيارة عرفات للمغرب في إطار جَوْلة تشمل عددا من العواصم العربية.

٦ـ غادر تونس وَفْدٌ من مُنَظَّمَة التحرير الفلسطينية اول من امس الخميس متوجّها الى طَهُران. ويرأس الوفد الشيخ عبد الحميد السائح رئيس المَجْلِس الوطني الفلسطيني.

٧ـ وصل الى موسكو امس في زيارة هي الاولى من نوعها وفد المجاهدين الأفْغان برئاسة زعيمهم بُرهان الدين ربّاني.

٨ـ يصل الى صنعاء في الايام القليلة القادمة وفد كويتي يضمّ عددا من الشَّخْصِيَّات السياسية والفِكْرية † .

٩ـ علمت "الشرق الاوسط" ان الرئيس التونسي زين العابدين بن علي سيصل القاهرة خلال شهر نوفمبر الجاري في زيارة رسمية تستغرق عدة ايام على رأس وفد يضم عددا من المسؤولـين التونسيين .

١٠ـعلم في جدّة امس ان وزير الهاتف السوري سيصل الى السعودية يوم الاحد المقبل في زيارة خاطفة تستغرق خمس ساعات .

١١ـعبد الحميد العبيدي رئيس تحرير مَجَلَّة "الحَضارة والإعْلام" الليبية يزور الاحد المقبل جامعة الملك سعود في الرياض .

١٢ـوصل وزير الدفاع الامريكي المنامة امس قادما من سلطنة عمان في إطار جَوْلة في منطقة الخليج تشمل ايضا المملكة العربية السعودية والكويت .

١٣ـيصل الى القاهرة غدا الجمعة زعيم حزب الشعب الديمقراطي السوداني وزعيم المعارضة على رأس وَفْد يضمّ عددا من الشخصيات والأحزاب الجنوبية في زيارة الى مصر تستغرق عدة ايام .

١٤ـوليد الحسيني رئيس تحرير مجلة "الكِفاح العربي" عاد الى بيروت بعد جولة شملت عدة عواصم عربية .

١٥ـ غادر الرئيس المصري حسني مبارك جدّة في الساعة الرابعة من مساء امس بعد زيارة للمملكة العربية السعودية لم يُعلَن عنها سابقا.

---

†The word *shakhṣiyyah*, originally an abstract noun, continues to be treated grammatically as if it denoted an object rather than a person, even in contexts such as the above.

١٦ـ وصل الى واشنطن امس السيد فؤاد سلطان وزير السِّياحة والطَّيَران المَدَنيّ المصري في اختتام زيارة عمل استمرّت أسبوعا.

١٧ـ وصل علي أكبر ولايتي وزير الخارجية الإيراني صباح امس الى فيينا في زيارة رسمية للنَّمْسا تستمر يومين .

١٨ـ وصل الأمير عبد الله بن عبد العزيز وليّ العَهْد ونائب رئيس مجلس الوزراء ورئيس الحَرَس الوطني السعودي الى الدار البيضاء مساء امس في زيارة خاصة للمغرب تستغرق يومين.

١٩ـ عاد الى عَمّان بعد ظهر امس العاهل الأُرْدُنّيّ الملك حسين قادما من مسقط بعد زيارة لسلطنة عمان استغرقت يومين .

٢٠ـ توجّه السفير عبد المحسن الجيعان مندوب الكويت الدائم في الجامعة العربية الى بلاده في زيارة خاصة تستغرق يومين يعود بعدها الى القاهرة .

CLASSROOM PRACTICE

2.1.1 Written Exercise

Referring to examples 1–10 above, use each of the following words/phrases in a complete Arabic sentence of your own:

قادماً مِن ـ آتياً مِن ـ مُتَوَجِّهاً إلى ـ عَدَدُ مِن ـ عِدَّةُ ... ـ بِضْعُ/بِضْعَةُ ... ـ في إطار ... ـ زِيارةٌ خاطفةٌ ـ ضَمَّ ـ رَأْسَ

2.1.2 Written Exercise

Referring to examples 11–20 above, use each of the following words/phrases in a complete Arabic sentence of your own:

عَادَ مِن ـ عَادَ إلى ـ اِسْتَمَرَّ ـ زِيارةُ عَمَلٍ ـ تَوَجَّهَ إلى

2.1.3 Written Exercise

1. Listen to sentences from examples 1–10 being read aloud at dictation speed by the teacher. As you listen, write an English translation of the sentences.
2. Listen to the same sentences being read aloud again, and write them down in Arabic. Compare your versions with the printed text.

2.1.4 *Written Exercise*

1. Listen to sentences from examples 11–20 being read aloud at dictation speed by the teacher. As you listen, write an English translation of the sentences.

2. Listen to the same sentences being read aloud again, and write them down in Arabic. Compare your versions with the printed text.

HOMEWORK EXERCISES

1. Compile a list of the new Arabic names of cities and countries and adjectives of nationality used in Lesson 2.1.

2. Written translation of examples 1–10.

*3. Written translation of examples 11–20.

4. Use each of the following words/phrases in a complete Arabic sentence of your own:

مُنَظَّمَةُ التحريرِ الفلسطينيةُ ـ المَجْلِسُ الوطنيّ الفلسطينيّ ـ مُجاهِدٌ ـ شَخْصِيَّةٌ ـ مَسْؤُولٌ

*5. Use each of the following words/phrases in a complete Arabic sentence of your own:

وزيرُ السِّياحة ـ وزيرُ الطَّيَران ـ وليُّ عَهْدٍ ـ الجامعة العربية ـ مَنْدوبٌ

6. Write an Arabic news story of your own containing the following words/phrases in any order you wish:

أمينٌ عامٌّ ـ زيارةٌ لم يُعْلَن عنها سابقا ـ حِزْبٌ ـ اشْتِراكيٌّ ـ شَعْبيٌّ

LESSON 2.2: MESSAGES, RECEPTIONS AND MEETINGS

● **Messages**

Many short front-page articles and Arab affairs items concern the delivery of personal messages from one head of government to another. The contents of such messages are not reported verbatim and are seldom discussed.

Below are examples of some of the commonest expressions used in connection with messages. Study the examples and translate them orally before doing the Classroom Practice.

Examples

- رسالة لـ لعاهل الاردني مِن الرئيس المصري

- تَلَقَّى الأمير عبد الله بن عبد العزيز وليّ العَهْد ونائب رئيس مَجْلِس الوزراء ورئيس الحَرَس الوطني السعودي رسالةً مِن الرئيس المصري .

- تلقَّى الرئيس حسني مبارك امس رسالةً شَفَوِيَّةً مِن أمير دولة البحرين .

- تلقَّى العاهل الاردني رسالةً خَطِّيَّةً مِن الرئيس المصري نَقَلَها السفير المصري .

- تَسَلَّمَ خادم الحَرَمَيْنِ الشَّريفَيْنِ الملك فَهْد بن عبد العزيز اَل سعود رسالةً مِن العاهل الإسباني و سلَّم الرسالةَ لـ خادم الحرمين الشريفين السفير الإسباني .

- تسلَّم أمير دولة البحرين الشيخ عيسى بن سلْمان اَل خليفة رسالةً خَطية مِن الرئيس الامريكي تتعلَّق بـ العَلاقات الثُّنائِيّ بين البلدين . و سلَّم الرسالةَ وزير الدفاع الامريكي .

> Note that the first example is in the style of a headline.
> Note that in the last two examples, the style $\bar{A}l$ ($=ahl$, '(of the)
> family/house of') should not be confused with the article.

CLASSROOM PRACTICE

2.2.1 Oral Exercise

Translate the following sentences into Arabic:

1. Prince Charles has received a personal message from the King of Spain.
2. The Kuwaiti papers report that the Iranian Deputy Foreign Minister is currently in Bahrain as part of a two-week official tour of the Gulf region.
3. Our Tripoli correspondent reports the arrival in Libya of the leader of the Sudanese People's Democratic Party on a surprise visit.
4. The Egyptian President has received a written message from the Emir of Bahrain about bilateral relations between the two countries.
5. The King of Jordan has received a verbal message from the Saudi Crown Prince concerning the two countries' relations.
6. The Iranian officials arrived in Muscat at five o'clock yesterday afternoon at the head of a delegation comprising a number of important Iranians.
7. The General Secretary of the Socialist Party will lead a delegation consisting of a number of intellectuals.
8. The ruler of Bahrain yesterday received a message from King Hussein of Jordan which was delivered by the Jordanian ambassador.
9. The former French prime minister has decided to postpone her visit to Rabat.
10. The US ambassador arrived in Casablanca yesterday on his way to Tunis; before leaving, he gave the King of Morocco a message from the president.
11. Yesterday, the Kuwaiti ambassador arrived in Muscat from Cairo, where he delivered a written message from the Emir of Kuwait to Egypt's President Mubarak.
12. The American Defense Secretary has arrived in Casablanca from Tunis as part of a tour of the region which will last for several days and include Rabat and Algiers.
13. The Saudi ambassador returned to Cairo yesterday with (= carrying) a message from the Saudi King to President Mubarak.
14. The King of Morocco was given a letter from the King of Saudi Arabia by the Saudi ambassador.

15. The Saudi ambassador has delivered a message from King Fahd to King Hussein of Jordan; the message is said to concern relations between the two countries.

16. Yasser Arafat, leader of the PLO, will be arriving in Tunis on a flying visit in the course of the next few days.

17. PLO leader Yasser Arafat will be leading the Palestinian delegation, which will be arriving in Cairo in the course of the month.

18. PLO leader Yasser Arafat will be arriving in Cairo in the course of the month at the head of a Palestinian delegation as part of a tour of the region which will include the Egyptian, Tunisian and Jordanian capitals.

19. Yasser Arafat's Cairo visit will be the first of its kind since the Gulf War.

20. The Afghan mujahideen delegation has arrived in Moscow on the first visit of its kind to the Russian capital.

2.2.2 *Written Exercise*

Listen to sentences from 2.2.1 Oral Exercise being read aloud at dictation speed by the teacher. As you listen, write an Arabic translation of the sentences.

● **Receptions and meetings**

Like the delivery of messages, reports of official receptions and meetings figure prominently on the front pages of Arabic newspapers and in broadcast news bulletins. Such reports often constitute complete news items, no comment being made on the significance of the meeting; the outcome of the meeting may or may not be reported. For examples of reports which record both the meeting and its outcome, see Unit 3, Lesson 3.3.

Examples

ـ اسْتقْبل العاهل الاردني السفيرَ الامريكي .

ـ صرح الرئيس المصري بأنه ـــ سيلتقي بـــ العاهل المغربي بعد يومين ، واكد ايضا انه ـــ سيلتقي مع وزير الخارجية المغربي.

ـ علم في الرباط ان وزير الخارجية الاسباني **كان سيستقبل**
العاهلَ المغربي الملك الحسن الثاني ثم **يلتقي** بعد ذلك **بـ** وزير
الخارجية المغربي. و **سيلتقي** وزير الخارجية الاسباني في مدريد
مع مسؤول العلاقات الخارجية في جَبْهة البوليساريو .

Note the two constructions of *iltaqā* in the second example; the
second is not given in Hans Wehr's *Dictionary of Modern
Written Arabic*. New preposition constructions of this type
occur frequently in Media Arabic; many of them are not listed
in dictionaries.
Note the difference between the meanings/translations of
istaqbala in the first and third examples.

CLASSROOM PRACTICE

2.2.3 Comprehension Exercise

To the non-Arab listener, some Arabic names may sound ambiguous (cf.
English names such as King, Lord, Major) and may be difficult to detach
from their context.

Listen to the following passages, each of which will be read aloud twice
by the teacher. Summarise each passage in English, distinguishing
between personal names and official titles.

١ـ تلقى الرئيس المصري حسني مبارك امس رسالة شفوية من
الشيخ عيسى بن سلمان آل خليفة امير دولة البحرين .

٢ـ تسلم الشيخ خليفة بن حمد آل ثاني امير دولة قطر رسالة من
الملك خوان كارلوس ملك اسبانيا. وسلم الرسالة لأمير دولة قطر
وزير الشؤون الخارجية الاسباني .

٣ـ تلقى السُّلطان قابوس بن سعيد سلطان عمان رسالة من
الرئيس الايراني نقلها نائب وزير الخارجية الايراني الذي يزور
مسقط حاليا واستقبله السلطان قابوس امس .

٤ـ استقبل الامير سلطان بن عبد العزيز النائب الثاني لرئيس مجلس الوزراء ووزير الدفاع والطيران السعودي في مكتبه بالرياض امس وزيرالدولة للشؤون الخارجية بسّلطنة عمان السيد يوسف بن علوي بن عبد الله . وكان السيد يوسف بن علوي قد وصل الى الرياض في وقت سابق امس .

٥ـ استقبل الرئيس اليمني علي عبد الله صالح ونائبه علي سالم البيض بعد ظهر امس السيد عبد العزيز الرواس وزير الإعلام في سلطنة عمان. وذكرت اذاعة صنعاء ان المسؤول العماني نقل الى الرئيس اليمني رسالة من السلطان قابوس تتعلق بالعلاقات الثنائية بين البلدين .

HOMEWORK

1. Compile a list of the new Arabic names of cities and countries and adjectives of nationality used in Lesson 2.2.
2. Written translation of any five sentences from 2.2.1 Oral Exercise.
3. Write an Arabic news story of your own containing the following words/phrases in any order you wish:

ـ وَفْدٌ ـ وزيرُ الإعْلام ـ جَبْهةُ البوليساريو ـ رِسالةٌ تتعلق بِ ـ في وقتٍ سابقٍ

4. Study sentences 2 and 4 in 2.2.3 Comprehension Exercise. Both contain unnecessary repetitions.
   (a) Rewrite the sentences, avoiding the repetitions.
   (b) Name the construction(s) you have used in doing so.
5. Compile a list of the expressions of date and time used in Units 1 and 2, giving a brief context for each.

Problems of Comprehension

A prominent feature of Media Arabic is the use of *variation* – as when different forms of a title are used – and *padding* – as when names and titles are repeated unnecessarily. Both procedures may be considered extensions of Media Arabic's reliance on synonyms.

Initially, this use of synonyms, variation and padding may impede comprehension, especially aural comprehension. Like synonyms, however, variations and padding generally occur in predictable slots. If the function of a slot is known, the meaning of its contents can usually be guessed.

This unit describes some of the commonest forms of padding, with the aim of increasing the learner's stock of small 'units of comprehension', and of encouraging intelligent guesswork at the meaning of unfamiliar items occupying familiar slots.

From the point of view of translation, careful consideration should be given to the examples of padding/synonyms and variation given in Lessons 3.1–3.3 below, and to the advantages, or in some cases disadvantages, which these features may offer to the translator, particularly the oral translator.

LESSON 3.1: SYNONYMS AND PADDING

- *Qāma bi-* + *maṣdar* as an all-purpose synonym of active verbs
  Qāma bi- (general sense: 'to do/make') occurs frequently in both Modern Standard Arabic and Media Arabic as a simple verb. For example:

$$\text{. تقوم ربّة البيت بـ أشغال المنزل}$$

$$\text{ـ قال الرئيس وهو يعلن برنامج اصلاحات انه من المستحيل ان}$$
$$\text{تقوم الحكومة بـ كل شيء .}$$

In Media Arabic, however, *qāma bi-* occurs much more frequently in combination with the *maṣdar* of another verb. When so used, it may provide solutions to a number of problems of construction, and lends itself to a variety of translations, according to context.

Compare

$$\text{يذكر مراسلنا ان الرئيس المصري يزور منطقة الخليج}$$

and

$$\text{يذكر مراسلنا ان الرئيس المصري يقوم بـ زيارة رسمية لمنطقة}$$
$$\text{الخليج.}$$

The use of *qāma bi-* + *maṣdar* in the second example makes it possible to specify, using a verb, that the visit is official, and yields several English translations.

The *qāma bi-* + *maṣdar* construction is also widely employed in Media Arabic even when the use of the simple verb presents no difficulties. It is then, structurally, no more than padding, the construction being equivalent to a synonym of the verb to which the *maṣdar* belongs. Here again, the context will suggest the appropriate English translation.

- *Tamma* + *maṣdar* as an all-purpose synonym of passive verbs
  The verb *tamma* is passive in sense, though its vowelling is that of an active verb. Like *qāma bi-*, it may occur in Media Arabic as a simple verb (general sense: 'to be done/made/concluded'). For example:

$$\text{. تمّت الدَّوْرَةُ الأُولى لِلَّجْنَة}$$

Just as frequently, it is used, like *qāma bi-*, in combination with the *maṣdar* of another verb. This construction is equivalent to a synonym of the passive of the verb to which the *maṣdar* belongs, and context will suggest the best way to translate it. For example:

سيتِمّ غدا تَوْقيعُ اتِّفاقيّةٍ تِجاريّةٍ بين البلدين

will frequently be found in place of

سَتُوَقَّعُ غدا اتِّفاقيّةٌ تِجاريّةٌ بين البلدين

and could, in the absence of a wider context, be translated as if the ordinary passive had been used. In an example such as

تمّ الاتِّفاقُ على إرْسالِ وفْدٍ الى المُؤْتَمَر

the combination *tamma* + *maṣdar* could be translated impersonally ('it was agreed'), or by a phrase such as 'agreement was reached', or even 'they agreed', depending on the wider context.

CLASSROOM PRACTICE

3.1.1 Written Exercise

1. Listen to the following sentences, which will be read aloud twice at dictation speed by the teacher. As you listen, write an English translation of the sentences.
2. Listen to the same sentences being read aloud again, and write them down in Arabic, eliminating *qāma bi-* and *tamma* wherever possible.

١ـ تلقى العاهل الاردني رسالة خطية من الرئيس المصري قام بنقلها السفير المصري .

٢ـ تسلم خادم الحرمين الشريفين الملك فهد بن عبد العزيز آل سعود رسالة من العاهل الاسباني قام بتسليمها السفير الاسباني .

٣ـ تلقى السلطان قابوس بن سعيد سلطان عمان رسالة من الرئيس الايراني قام بنقلها نائب وزير الخارجية الايراني الذي يقوم حاليا بزيارة لمسقط .

٤ـ علمت "الشرق الاوسط" ان الرئيس التونسي سيقوم خلال الشهر الجاري بزيارة رسمية للقاهرة تستمر عدة ايام .

٥ـ تمت الدورة الاولى للجنة وتم خلالها الاتفاق على توقيع الاتفاقية التجارية الجديدة .

● **Synonyms of *wa-* and *fa-***

In Modern Standard Arabic, the coordinating particles *wa-* and *fa-* may be used to express relationships of simultaneity (*wa-*), consecutiveness, cause and effect, etc. (both *wa-* and *fa-*) existing between clauses, sentences and paragraphs.

In Media Arabic, *wa-* retains these functions, in particular that of introducing temporal and explanatory *ḥāls*, However, *wa-* is also often replaced or reinforced in ways such as the following:

wa- or *wa-* ... *ayḍan* may be replaced by *ka-mā*, when more than one action by the same person or of the same kind is being reported:

استقبل الدكتور بُطْرُس غالي الأمين العامّ للأُمَم المتحدة امس سفير المملكة المتحدة لَدَى الأُمَم المتحدة **كما** استقبل الدكتور غالي رئيس اللجنة الافريقية لحقوق الإنسان والشعوب الذي يزور نيو يورك حاليا .

wa- alone may be reinforced, padded or replaced by a variety of phrases which, though giving an impression of greater or more specific emphasis, may not require translation:

تلقى الرئيس المصري حسني مبارك رسالة من الشيخ خليفة بن حمد آل ثاني امير دولة قطر قام بتسليمها سفير قطر في القاهرة خلال استقبال الرئيس مبارك له امس . (و) **جَديرٌ بالذِكْر** أنّ امير قطر سيبدأ يوم الاثنين المقبل زيارة رسمية لمصر تَستغرِق أربعة أيام .

The explanatory or correlative functions of *fa-*, or of *wa-* introducing a *ḥāl*, are often taken over by *ḥaythu* or *idh*:

زيارة وزير الاعلام السوري الى طرابلس هي الثانية التي يقوم بها الى ليبيا خلال الاسبوع ، **حَيْثُ** زار طرابلس يومَي ١٩ و ٢٠ ديسمبر الحالي .

The use of *fa-* is, of course, compulsory in the constructions 'as for ...' (*ammā* ... *fa-*), 'although/despite ... yet (*fa-*)' and (where appropriate) 'if ... then (*fa-*)', but *fa-* is not very frequently met with outside these constructions in ordinary news items.

● **Pure padding**

This may take the form of redundant emphasis, when a resumptive
wa-dhālika is prefixed to an explanatory phrase or clause:

قرّر وزير الخارجية الاسباني تأجيل زيارته الخاصة للمغرب
وذلك لأسباب شخصية

or of redundant coordination, when a functionless *wa-* is inserted
before the relative pronoun:

اعلن الدكتور عصْمت عبد المجيد نائب رئيس الوزراء ووزير
الخارجية المصريَ انه أطْلع مبْعوث صنْدوق النّقْد الدولي امس على
الاصلاحات الاقتصادية المصرية والتي اعتبرها المبعوث إيجابية
للغاية .

The phrase *kull(un)/(an)/(in)* min inserted before a sequence of two or
more names may be genuinely distributive or simply padding.

Compare

تسلم وزير الخارجية السعودي الامير سعود الفيصل† امس
صورة من أوْراق اعْتماد السفير التونسي الجديد لدَى السعودية.
وتسلم الامير سعود ايضا نُسَخا من أوراق اعتماد سفراء كل من
ايرلندا والمكيسك وفنلندا وأوروغواي الجدد في السعودية

and

صرح الرئيس الامريكي جورج بوش في مدريد بأن هَدَف مؤتمر
مدريد هو الوصول الى مُعاهَدات سلام بين إسرائيل و كل من
سوريّة والأردن ولبنان .

● **Meaningless variation**

As has already been observed, Media Arabic often uses variant
constructions of the same verb without any change in meaning.
Examples noted earlier include *waṣala / waṣala ilā* and *iltaqā / iltaqā
maʿa* . Another example which will have been observed is *aʿlana /
aʿlana ʿan* .

Some prepositions unattached to verbs may also be substituted for each
other, in specific contexts, with no change in meaning. Common examples
are *fī / bi, fī /ladā* and *ladā /ʿinda*, in contexts such as the following:

†The style *al-* (for *ibn*) is sometimes used in Saudi Arabia and the Gulf.

ـ استقبل الامير عبد الله بن عبد العزيز ولي العهد ونائب رئيس
مجلس الوزراء ورئيس الحرس الوطني السعودي في مكتبه،
بـ الرياض امس السفير التونسي الجديد لَدَى السعودية كما
استقبل سفراء كل من ايرلندا والمكسيك وفنلندا وأوروغواي
الجدد في السعودية .

ـ وصل الامير عبد الله بن عبد العزيز ولي العهد ونائب رئيس
مجلس الوزراء ورئيس الحرس الوطني السعودي الى الدار
البيضاء امس . وكان في استقبال الامير عِنْدَ وصوله الوزير الاول
المغربي ووالي مدينة الدار البيضاء الكُبْرى وسفير المملكة
العربية السعودية لَدَى المغرب وشخصيات مَدَنيّة وعَسْكَريّة .

ـ وصل الرئيس اليمني علي عبد الله صالح الى مصر أوائل
الأسبوع الحالي في زيارة رسمية . وكان في استقباله لَدَى
وصوله الرئيس المصري حسني مبارك ونائب رئيس الوزراء
المصري .

Note that another common type of padding is discussed in part
II on page 122.

Note that another common type of padding is discussed in part II on page 122.

CLASSROOM PRACTICE

3.1.2 Oral Exercise

Translate each of the following sentences into Arabic in as many different
ways as possible, with and without padding (including repetitions and
variants of titles):

1. President Mubarak is currently on an official visit to Uruguay.
2. The Saudi Crown Prince has decided to postpone his visit to Austria
   for personal reasons.
3. The Austrian ambassador to Saudi Arabia yesterday presented his
   credentials to King Fahd. He also presented a copy of his credentials
   to the Crown Prince this morning.
4. A new trade agreement has been signed between Finland and
   Ireland.

5. The Crown Prince yesterday received the new Mexican ambassador to Saudi Arabia and the head of the African Human Rights Committee at his office in Riyadh.

6. The last session of the committee, in the course of which an agreement was signed, ended today in Brussels.

7. The president told the UN Secretary-General that the aim of the conference was to arrive at peace treaties between Israel and Syria, Lebanon and Jordan respectively.

8. This is Arafat's second visit to Tunis this week.

9. This is the IMF envoy's third visit to Cairo this month; he has already met with President Mubarak twice this week.

10. The deputy prime minister said that he had informed the IMF envoy of the new economic policy, and that he had considered it extremely positive.

*3.1.3 Oral Exercise

Repeat the above exercise with the following sentences:

1. The president told our correspondent that he had told the IMF envoy about the new economic programme, which he thought extremely positive.

2. The deputy prime minister told the IMF envoy about the economic reform programme, which he thought most positive, and about President Mubarak's visit to Saudi Arabia next month.

3. A trade agreement is to be signed this month between Austria and Morocco.

4. It was agreed that the presidents of Germany and Tunisia should each be given a copy of the peace treaty.

5. The first session of the Human Rights Committee has ended with the signing of a new agreement.

6. President Bush's special envoy, who has already been to the Gulf twice this week, is to meet the Ruler of Qatar tomorrow.

7. President Bush's personal envoy to the Gulf, who arrived in Qatar yesterday, has given the Ruler a message from the president.

8. Yasser Arafat has arrived in Tunis, where he was to have met the president, who is on a lightning trip to Algeria.

9. The prime minister said that the government was reforming the economy, but that the government alone could not do everything.

10. Kuwait's permanent delegate to the Arab League will be arriving in Cairo tomorrow on his second trip this week to the Egyptian capital.

HOMEWORK

1. Compile a list of the new Arabic names of cities, conurbations and countries and adjectives of nationality used in Lesson 3.1.

2. Written translation of any five sentences from 3.1.2 Oral exercise (in both padded and unpadded versions).

*3. Written translation of any five sentences from 3.1.3 Oral Exercise (in both padded and unpadded versions).

4. Use each of the following words/phrases in a complete Arabic sentence of your own:

وال ـ الأُمَم المتّحدة ـ مُؤْتَمَرٌ ـ أوائلُ .... ـ مَدَنيٌّ ـ عَسْكَريٌّ ـ مُعاهَدَةُ سلامٍ ـ إيجابيٌّ ـ حُقوقُ الإنسان ـ مدينة لندن الكُبْرى

5. Write an Arabic news story of your own using the following words/ phrases in any order you wish:

اتّفق على ـ أطْلَعَ + ه + على ـ صنْدوقُ النَّقْد الدوليّ ـ تِجاريّ ـ دَوْرَةٌ ـ هَدَفٌ

LESSON 3.2: 'FRAMES'

The stereotyped formulae of which public statements and reports of statements largely consist can be divided into two groups: words/phrases which introduce or link statements ('frames'); and set phrases which occupy predictable slots within the statement itself ('fillings').

Familiar 'fillings' include phrases such as those underlined below:

ـ اكد وزير الخارجية البريطاني تقدير بلاده لـ جهود مصر من اجل السلام في الشرق الاوسط .

ـ تلقى الرئيس التونسي رسالة من الرئيس الجزائري تتعلق بالعلاقات الثنائية بين البلدين .

'Fillings' will be examined further in Lesson 3.3.

Examples of 'frames' include *qāla* and its synonyms/near-synonyms, and *wa-* and its synonyms and reinforcements. For example:

أكد وزير الخارجية البريطاني تقدير بلاده لجهود مصر من اجل السلام في الشرق الاوسط وفي هذا الصَّدَد دعا الى تَعاوُن الدول العربية .

● The following examples of 'frames' are connected with *different kinds of statement*. Read them aloud, analyse them and translate them orally.

ـ أُصْدَرَ الرئيس بَياناً اعلن فيه برنامج اصلاحات .

ـ رَدّاً على سؤالٍ من الصَّحَفيين قال الرئيس انه سيزور سوريا في المستقبل القريب .

ـ بَعَثَ رئيس الوزراء رَدَّهُ على مُقْتَرَحات الرئيس الرامية الى الاصلاح. ويذكر ان فَحْوَى رسالة رئيس الوزراء يتعلق بـ الإجراءات الاقتصادية .

ـ قال الرئيس في مؤتمر صَحَفيّ انه سيلتقي مع زعيم المعارضة و أُشارَ إلى احتمال لِقاء مع زُعماء كل الاحزاب المُعارِضة .

ـ في حديث أدلى به لِـ "الشرق الاوسط" قال الرئيس انه سيلتقي مع زعيم المعارضة .

ـ في مقابلة مع "الشرق الأوسط" قال الرئيس انه سيلتقي مع زعيم المعارضة .

CLASSROOM PRACTICE

3.2.1 Written Exercise

1. Referring to the examples above, use each of the following words/ phrases in a complete Arabic sentence of your own:

مؤتمرٌ صَحَفيٌّ ـ أصْدَرَ بَياناً ـ فَحْوَى ـ إجْراءٌ ـ مُقابَلَةٌ

2. Referring to the examples above, write an Arabic news story of your own using the following words/phrases in any order you wish:

أدْلَى بِحديثٍ لِ ـ أشارَ إلى ـ رامٍ إلى ـ مُقْتَرَحاتٌ

● The following examples of 'frames' are connected with different *sources of information*. Read them aloud, analyse them and translate them orally.

١ـ لندن ـ وكالات الأنباء ـ اعلن قصر بكنجام امس ان الملكة إليزابيث ستقوم بأول زيارة دولة لألمانيا الموحّدة في اكتوبر من العام الجاري .

٢ـ أفادت الأنباء الواردة من بيروت بأنّ سليم الحص رئيس وزراء لبنان اعلن عن استقالة حكومته .

٣ـ أورّدت الصُّحُف اللبنانية أنّ ١٥٠ رجل أعْمال وشخصية سياسية وخبير اقتصادي من الدول العربية شاركوا في الدورة الرابعة والسبعين لاتّحاد غُرَف التجارة والصناعة والزراعة العربية .

٤ـ تشير معلوماتٌ غيرُ رسميةٍ إلى أن وزير الهاتف السوري سيصل إلى السعودية يوم الأحد المقبل في زيارة خاطفة .

٥ـ قال مُراقبون في الجزائر ان الحكومة الجزائرية تعمل على حلّ الأزْمة بينها وبين تونس .

٦ـ اكد مُتَحَدِّثٌ باسم منظمة التحرير الفلسطينية لـــوكالة "فرانس برس" ان الرئيس الفلسطيني ياسر عرفات تلقى دعوات رسمية لزيارة كل من سورية ومصر والاردن . وكان مسؤول فلسطيني كبير ذكر سابقا ان عرفات سيزور دمشق في الاسبوع القادم ، ويذكر ان هذه الزيارة هي الاولى لعرفات الى العاصمة السورية منذ الزيارة القصيرة التي قام بها في ابريل ١٩٨٨ .

٧ـ اعلن ناطقٌ باسم الشُّرْطة الاسرائيلية ان سائحة قتلت بعد ظهر امس في مدينة القدس القديمة .

٨ـ علمت "الشرق الاوسط" من مَصادرَ مُطَّلعةٍ ان الرئيس التونسي سيصل القاهرة خلال شهر نوفمبر الجَاريَّ في زيارة رسمية تستغرق عدة ايام على رأس وفد يضم عددا من المسؤولين التونسيين .

٩ـ الكويت ـ ق ـ ن ـ أ : اعلنت مصادرُ عالية ُ المُسْتَوَى في الجيش الكويتي امس ان المُناوَرات العسكرية الكويتية الامريكية المُشْتَرَكَة التي تجري حاليا تستمر حتى ٢١ نوفمبر الحالي .

١٠ـ ذكرت مصادرُ مَوْثوقُ بها ان الاجتماع بين رئيس الوزراء الباكستاني وزعماء المجاهدين الافغان الذي استغرق اربع ساعات انتهى بالاتفاق على ارسال وفد من المجاهدين الى موسكو في الاسبوع الاول من الشهر المقبل .

CLASSROOM PRACTICE

*3.2.2 *Written/Oral Exercise*

1. Using 'frames' from the examples given above, write four brief Arabic news stories of your own. Each should include the words/phrases given in one of groups (a)–(d) below.
2. Take it turns to read your own stories aloud and to translate each other's stories orally.

(a)

دَعْوَةٌ ـ أَلْمَانيا المُوَحَّدَةُ ـ مَسؤُولٌ كبيرٌ ـ لِقاءٌ ـ انتهى بـ

(b)

وَفْدٌ ـ حِزْبٌ مُعَارِضٌ ـ اسْتِقالَةٌ ـ أَزْمَةٌ ـ عَمِلَ على

(c)

شَارَكَ في ـ مُنَاوَرَةٌ ـ جَرَى ـ اِحْتِمالٌ ـ تَعَاوُنٌ

(d)

شُرْطَةٌ ـ قَتَلَ ـ سائِحٌ ـ رَجُلُ أَعْمالٍ ـ خَبيرٌ

3.2.3 Oral Exercise

Translate the following sentences into Arabic:

1. The president issued a statement calling for cooperation between Arab states.
2. Replying to journalists, the Russian president confirmed that he would be meeting the Afghan mujahideen delegation the next day.
3. At a press conference, high-ranking Foreign Office officials confirmed that the Queen had been invited to Germany in September.
4. Israel has not yet replied to the president's Middle East peace proposals; observers in Jerusalem say that the Israeli parliament may call for an official statement.
5. Informed sources in Lebanon say that the prime minister will announce his government's resignation tomorrow.
6. In an interview with the BBC, the prime minister referred to the opposition's economic programme and said that the government was working to resolve the current crisis.
7. A police spokesman announced that two businessmen killed in Belfast yesterday had been taking part in a conference at the Chamber of Commerce.
8. Reports from Amman say that the conference has ended with an agreement to send a delegation to the Arab League.

9. It is reported unofficially that joint US-Saudi manoeuvres in the Gulf could continue until the end of the month.
10. Reliable sources in Paris say that the Tunisian ambassador has delivered to the French Foreign Ministry a letter from the Tunisian president which is believed to concern political developments in Algeria.

3.2.4 Oral Exercise

Translate the following sentences into Arabic:

1. Informed sources say that China has agreed to send a number of military experts to Iraq.
2. A UN spokesman said that UN Secretary-General Boutros Ghali would be issuing a statement in a few hours' time.
3. A police spokesman confirmed that the two businessmen killed in Belfast yesterday had been attending a conference at the Chamber of Commerce.
4. Highly-placed sources in the Foreign Office say that the meeting in Brussels between the Foreign Secretary and the French Agriculture Minister may be postponed.
5. Observers in Algiers say there is a possibility that the president will meet opposition leaders tomorrow.
6. A British army spokesman said yesterday that there was a possibility that joint manoeuvres with Kuwait would have to be postponed.
7. Replying to journalists, the Foreign Secretary said that the government was working to resolve the current crisis in Yugoslavia, and called for European cooperation.
8. Unofficial reports from Tunis say that a delegation of Algerian intellectuals will be arriving in the Tunisian capital tomorrow to take part in a conference on human rights.
9. A UN spokeswoman said that the Secretary-General would send his reply to the Israeli proposals at the beginning of next month.
10. Reliable sources in Paris say that yesterday's three-hour meeting between French Agriculture Ministry officials and a high-ranking Moroccan delegation ended in the signing of a trade agreement between the two countries.

HOMEWORK

1. Translate the following sentence into Arabic:

According to reliable sources in Paris, a letter from the Tunisian president delivered yesterday to the French Foreign Ministry by the Tunisian ambassador is believed to concern political developments in Algeria.

What adjustments to the English order of presentation or additions to the English text must you make in order for the passage to conform to the style of the examples of Media Arabic with which you are familiar?

2. Written translation of any five sentences from 3.2.3 Oral Exercise.
*3. Written translation of any five sentences from 3.2.4 Oral Exercise.
4. Use each of the following words/phrases in a complete Arabic sentence of your own:

حَلَّ ـ تَعَاوَنَ (مع) ـ اِحْتَمَلَ ـ وَثِقَ بِ ـ اِسْتَقَالَ

REVISION

*3.2.5 *Written Exercise*

Listen to sentences from 3.2.3 Oral Exercise and/or 3.2.4 Oral Exercise which will be read aloud at dictation speed by the teacher. As you listen, write an Arabic translation of the sentences.

LESSON 3.3: 'FRAMES' AND 'FILLINGS'

- The following examples of 'frames' are connected with different *circumstances giving rise to statements/reports*: meetings, conferences, negotiations and discussions. Read them aloud, analyse and translate them orally.

ـ عَقَدَ الرؤساء الاوروبيون اجتماعاً في باريس وسوف يَنْعَقِدُ اجتماعٌ ثانٍ في العاصمة الفرنسية بعد شهرين .

ـ عُقِدَ مُوْتَمَرُ السلامِ في مدريد .

ـ تم الاتفاق على عَقْدِ مُؤْتَمَرِ قِمَّةٍ في واشنطن .

ـ رحّبت مصادر دبلوماسية خليجية في الكويت امس باحتمال تأجيل مَوْعِد الاجتماعِ التركيِّ ـ البلغاريِّ المُقَرَّرِ عَقْدُهُ في الكويت أواخِرَ الشهر الحالي إلى وقت آخر خلال الشهر المقبل.

ـ تم الاتفاق على إنهاء الحرب بعد مُفاوَضاتٍ قَادَها مُمَثِّلُ الأُمَم المتحدة .

ـ حَضَرَ الاجتماعَ مُمَثِّلُ منظمة التحرير الفلسطينية ومُمَثِّلو كل من مصر وسوريا والاردن. وتم خلال الاجتماع بَحْثُ القضية الفلسطينية والعلاقات بين الدول العربية .

ـ استمرّت المُباحَثاتُ حَوْلَ القضيةِ الفلسطينيةِ والعلاقات بين الدول العربيه عدة ساعات .

ـ سيُناقِشُ الرؤساءُ العرب خلال اجتماعهم القضيةَ الفلسطينيةَ.

ـ وزير الدفاع السوري سيُجْري مُناقَشاتٍ مع منظمة التحرير الفلسطينية حَوْلَ القضية الفلسطينية .

ـ اِسْتَعْرَضَ الرئيسان التونسي والفرنسي خلال اجتماعهما آخر تطوّراتِ الأحْداث في الجزائر .

ـ تم خلال الاجتماع اِسْتِعْراضُ آخر تطوّرات الأحْداث فى الجزائر و تَناوَلَ الحديثُ ايضا القضية الفلسطينية والعلاقاتِ بين البلدين .

CLASSROOM PRACTICE

3.3.1 Oral Exercise

Translate the following sentences into Arabic:

1. Discussions lasted for three days.
2. A conference is to be held in Damascus to discuss human rights in the Middle East.
3. Representatives from Egypt, Jordan and the PLO will take part in the discussions.
4. Representatives from several Arab countries will attend the conference, which is to be held in Damascus.
5. The conference which was to have been held in Brussels next month has been postponed; European foreign ministers have welcomed the postponement.
6. The negotiations, which lasted two years and were conducted by the UN Secretary-General's representative, ended today with the signing of a peace treaty.
7. The French Foreign Minister is to hold talks with the Tunisian Foreign Minister.
8. The two Foreign Ministers will review the latest developments in Algeria.
9. Talks were held during which the French and Tunisian foreign Ministers reviewed the latest developments in Algeria. The talks also dealt with the Palestinian question and the peace conference.
10. Replying to journalists, the prime minister said it was possible that a summit meeting might be called in the near future.

*3.3.2 Oral Exercise

Translate the following passage into Arabic, section by section:

A French Foreign Ministry spokeswoman has announced / the postponement until September of talks which were to have been held in the French capital this month / to discuss the latest developments in the former Soviet Union. / At a press conference, the Foreign Ministry spokeswoman confirmed / that the Polish prime minister would be a participant in the talks, / and she also confirmed that a meeting would take place in Paris between the French and Polish Foreign Ministers / in advance of the European summit which is scheduled to take place in Brussels next month. / According to diplomatic sources, the French Ministry of Agriculture is working to resolve the trade crisis between France and Poland. / The British and Irish governments have issued a joint statement calling for European cooperation / and, in a statement to the press this morning, the British Foreign Secretary said that his government would support joint European measures to resolve the crisis.

*3.3.3 Written Exercise

Listen to sentences from 3.3.1 Oral Exercise, which will be read aloud at dictation speed by the teacher. As you listen, write an Arabic translation of the sentences.

*3.3.4 Written Exercise

Listen to the passage from 3.3.2 Oral Exercise being read aloud, section by section, by the teacher. As you listen, write an Arabic translation of the passage.

● Below are a few examples of phrases, some of which are already familiar to you, which occur very frequently as *'fillings'* in reports of statements. Read them aloud; analyse and translate them orally:

- جرى خلال الاجتماع   تَبادُلُ الآراءِ .

- جرى خلال الاجتماع   تَبادُلُ وُجْهاتِ النَّظَرِ .

ـ جرى خلال الاجتماع استعراض آخِر تطوّرات الأحْداث على الساحة الدولية وتناول الحديثُ ايضاً الأمورَ ذاتَ الاهتمام المُشتَرك و الأمورَ التي تَهُمّ الرؤساءَ العربَ . و على صعيدٍ آخَر تم استعراض المُسْتَجِدّات الافريقية و مُستَجِدّات الأوْضاعِ في أوروبا الشرقية .

> Note that *jarā* is used interchangeably with *tamma* in the above examples.

CLASSROOM PRACTICE

3.3.5 *Oral/ Written Exercise*

1. Read the following passages aloud and translate them orally, identifying stereotyped 'fillings'.
2. Taking any three passages as models, reuse at least one stereotyped component of each, whether 'frame' or 'filling', in three complete written Arabic sentences of your own.
*3. Take it in turns to read your own sentences aloud and to translate each other's sentences orally.

١ـ اجتـمـع نائـب رئيس الوزراء لشـؤون الأمْن والدفاع في سلطنة عمان امس مع وزير الدفاع بجمـهورية الصومال الديمقراطية . وجري خلال اللقاء استعراض وجهات النظر حول الأمور ذات الاهتمام المشترك والعلاقات الثنائية بين البلدين . وكان الوزير الصومالي قد وصل إلى مسقط يوم الأربعاء الماضي .

٢ـ تلقى الشيخ خليفة بن حمد آل ثاني أمير دولة قطر رسالة شفوية من الرئيس المصري حسني مبارك تتعلق بالعلاقات بين البلدين وسبُل تعزيزها ودعْمها في إطار العمل العربي المشترك . وقام بنقل الرسالة وزير الداخلية المصري الذي يزور الدَّوْحة حاليا خلال استقبال أمير دولة قطر له أمس . ومن جهةٍ أُخْرى اجتمع وزير الداخلية القطري صباح أمس مع وزير الداخلية المصري وتم خلال الاجتماع بحث العلاقات الثنائية بين البلدين وسبل تعزيزها وتطويرها .

٣ـ اعلن السيد خالد الحسن امس ان منظمة التحرير الفلسطينية بعثت الى واشنطن امس ردها على مقترحاتها الرامية الى اجراء محادثات في القاهرة بين وفدين اسرائيلي وفلسطيني . وأضاف السيد خالد الحسن ان المنظمة بعثت بردها الى الحكومة المصرية لتنقلها الى الولايات المتحدة وذلك بعد مناقشة الإيضاحات الأمريكية التي تلقتها في وقت سابق . وردا على سؤال عن فحوى الرد قال : اننا دائما نتّخذ مَوْقفا إيجابيا ولكننا نَرْفُضُ الاتجاهَ السَّلْبيَّ للآخَرين .

٤ـ استقبل الشيخ حمد بن عيسى آل خليفة أمير دولة البحرين أمس السيد محمود عباس (أبو مازن†) عُضْو اللجنة التَّنْفيذيّة لمنظمة التحرير الفلسطينية وعُضْو اللجنة المَرْكَزيّة لحركة التحرير الوطني الفلسطيني "فتح" الذي يزور المنامة حاليا . وتم خلال المقابلة استعراض آخر التطورات على الساحتين العربية والفلسطينية خاصّةً ما يتعلق بالاْنْتِفاضة الفلسطينية في الأراضي المُحْتَلَّة إضافةً إلى مستجدات الأوَضاع في المنظمة . ويذكر ان زيارة أبو مازن† للمنامة تأتي في إطار جولة له في عدد من دول المنطقة حيث كان قد زار الدوحة قبل ذلك .

٥ـ استقبل الشيخ خليفة بن حمد آل خليفة امير دولة قطر صباح امس الامين العام لمجلس التعاون لدول الخليج العربية . وتناول الحديث خلال المقابلة عددا من الامور التي تهم مجلس التعاون الخليجي وسبل تطوير وتَنْميَة علاقات التعاون†† بين الدول الأَعْضاء وسبل التعاون بينها في المَجالات الإسلامية .

٦ـ استقبل الرئيس المصري حسني مبارك امس وزير الحَجّ السعودي الذي يزور القاهرة حاليا . وصرح المسؤول السعودي عَقِبَ المقابلة بأنه جري خلالها استعراض القضايا العربية . ومن ناحِيَته قال وزير الأوْقاف المصري للصحفيين بعد المقابلة ان الرئيس مبارك دعا الى المَزيد من التعاون بين الدول الإسلامية ودَعْم الدَّعْوة الإسلامية على المُسْتَوَيَيْنِ المَحَلّيّ والعالَميّ .

---

†Note the invariable form of the name
††The form taken here by the *iḍāfah* is very common in Media Arabic.

٧ـ قال الرئيس المصري في مؤتمر صحفي ان اجتماعه مع الرئيس السوري كان ناجحا وفي هذا الصدد دعا الى تعاون الدول العربية وقَدَّمَ إيضاحات حول مَوْقِف بلاده من المؤتمر الدولي للسلام في الشرق الاوسط .

٨ـ توجه الى ايران امس وفد برلماني مغربي للمشاركة في المؤتمر الدولي الخامس لِمُسانَدَة انتفاضة الشعب الفلسطيني. وفي تونس اعلن مصدر رسمي امس ان وفدا برئاسة سكرتير الدولة للشؤون الدينية السيد علي الشابي سيشارك في مؤتمر طهران . وكان الرئيس التونسي زين العابدين بن علي استقبل الشابي وحَمَّلَه رسالة الي نَظيره الايراني تتناول "علاقات الأُخُوَّة والتعاون" بين البلدين حَسْبَما أفاد المصدر .

٩ـ اكد مصدر مسؤول في وزرارة الخارجية المغربية لـ "الشرق الاوسط" ان وزراء الخارجية المَغاربيّين بحثوا خلال اجتماعهم الذي بدأ امس في مَرّاكُش المشاركة في المفاوضات المُتَعَدِّدَة الأطْراف التي سَتجرى في إطار المؤتمرالدولي للسلام . وأضاف المصدر نَفْسُهُ ان المسؤولين المغاربيّين المجتمعين بمراكش يعملون على الوصول الى موقف مشترك إزاءَ الخَطَوات المقبلة في مفاوضات السلام حول الشرق الاوسط .

١٠ـ ذكر بيان أصدره الأمين العام لمنظمة المؤتمرالإسلامي ان المؤتمر الوِزاري الإسلامي العشرين الذي عقد في اسطنبول في أغُسْطُس الماضي " أعرب عن تقديره ودعمه للجهود الجارية لإيجاد حلّ عادل وشامل ودائم للقضية الفلسطينية على أساس الشَّرْعيّة الدولية".

HOMEWORK

1. Use each of the following words/phrases in a complete Arabic sentence of your own:

رَحَّبَ بِ ـ أواخِرُ ... ـ حَضَرَ ـ القضية الفلسطينية ـ اتِّجاهٌ

*2. Written translation of 3.3.2 Oral Exercise.

3. Use each of the following words/phrases in a complete Arabic sentence of your own:

إزاءَ ـ عَقِبَ ـ ناجِحٌ ـ نَظيرُ ـ المَزيدُ من ـ دوليٌّ ـ مَحَلّيٌّ ـ
عالَميّ ـ مرْكَزيّ ـ عُضْوٌ

4. Write an Arabic news story of your own using the following words/phrases in any order you wish:

مُساندَةٌ ـ مجلسُ التعاونِ الخليجيّ ـ انْتِفاضَةٌ ـ أضافَ ـ
قَدَّمَ إيضاحاتٍ حَوْلَ ـ العَمَلُ العَرَبيُّ المُشْتَرَكُ ـ
مفاوضاتٌ مُتَعَدِّدَةُ الأطْرافِ ـ حَلٌّ عادلٌ وشاملٌ ودائمٌ ـ
رَفَضَ ـ سَلْبيٌّ

*5. Horoscopes are a daily feature in many Arabic newspapers. Find and translate your own horoscope from among the following:

الأبراج

الحمل   (٣/٢١ ـ ٤/١٩)
تقوم بخطوات ايجابية تقودك الى النجاح .

الثور   (٤/٢٠. ـ ٥/٢٠)
تحقق هدفا كنت تبذل مجهودا كبيرا لبلوغه .

الجوزاء   (٥/٢١ ـ ٦/٢٠)
تحصل على دعم معنوي كنت بحاجة اليه .

السرطان   (٦/٢١ ـ ٧/٢٢)
لا تهتم بما يقوله الحساد .

الأسد   (٧/٢٣ ـ ٨/٢٢)
عليك اتخاذ قرار سريع في شأن مشروع سفر .

العذراء   (٨/٢٣ ـ ٩/٢٢)

لا تتأخر في التعبير عن رأيك بصراحة إذا دعت الحاجة .

الميزان   (٩/٢٣ ـ ١٠/٢٢)

الصورة على الصعيد العاطفي تتوضح . تابع سعيك الى تحقيق أحلامك .

العقرب   (١٠/٢٣ ـ ١١/٢٠)

تقوم برحلة بعيدة .

القوس   (١١/٢١ ـ ١٢/٢٠)

معظم الأعمال التي تقوم بها هذه المدة سيكون ناجحا .

الجدي   (١٢/٢١ ـ ١/١٩)

لا تبذل مجهودا يفوق طاقتك على الصعيد المهني .

الدلو   (١/٢٠ ـ ٢/١٨)

لا تهمل احدى الفرص النادرة التي تجدها على الصعيد المهني .

الحوت   (١/١٩ ـ ٣/٢٠)

تعيش في سعادة تامة على الصعيد العاطفي فاعرف كيف تحافظ عليها .

LESSON 3.4: CUTTING THROUGH THE PADDING

Problems of comprehension, especially aural comprehension arise, when a news item consists entirely of padding and stereotyped 'fillings', making it difficult to identify salient points, and also when an item departs unexpectedly from the stereotype. Typical examples are given in the Classroom Practice below. Use these examples and your knowledge of 'frames' and 'fillings' to help develop a sense of the potential newsworthiness of a given item.

CLASSROOM PRACTICE

3.4.1 Written/Oral Exercise

1. Listen to the following story, which will be read aloud twice at dictation speed by the teacher. Summarise the passage in English in writing.
2. Listen to the same passage being read aloud again and write it down in Arabic. Resummarise it in English and compare your two summaries.
3. Compare your version of the passage with the version below. Translate the passage orally, identifying and discussing any points of difficulty.

أجرى خادم الحرمين الشريفين الملك فهد بن عبد العزيز آل سعود محادثات أمس مع الرئيس المصري حسني مبارك استعرضا خلالها المستجدات الإقليميّة والدولية . وكان الرئيس مبارك قد وصل إلى جدة في الساعة الرابعة من مساء أمس في زيارة للمملكة العربية السعودية ، وكان خادم الحرمين الشريفين في استقباله في مطار الملك عبد العزيز الدولي . كما كان في استقباله الأمير عبد الله بن عبد العزيز ولي العهد ونائب رئيس مجلس الوزراء ورئيس الحرس الوطني السعودي . وكان في استقبال الرئيس مبارك أيضا الأمير ماجد بن عبد العزيز أمير منطقة مكّة المُكَرَّمَة والأُمراء والوزراء وكبار المسؤولين من مدنيين وعسكريين وأعضاء سفارة مصر لدى السعودية. ويرافق الرئيس مبارك وزير الإعلام السيد صفوت الشريف ووزير التنمية الإدارية الدكتور عاطف عبيد ووزير المالية الدكتور محمد الرزاز ورئيس ديوان رئيس الجمهورية الدكتور زكريا عزمي ووكيل أول وزارة الخارجية ومدير مكتب الرئيس للشؤون السياسية الدكتور أسامة الباز .

وفي القاهرة اعتبرت الدوائر السياسية لقاء القمة بين الملك فهد والرئيس مبارك بالغ الأهمّية نَظَراً للعلاقات الوطيدة التي تربط بين الزعيمين والبلدين، ولأنه يأتي في وقت تتقارب فيه الخطوات لتحقيق الأهداف العربية والإسلامية العليا ، خاصةً في ما يتعلق بالتطورات السياسية للقضية الفلسطينية والمَجهودات العربية والدولية في هذا الصدد . كما تأتي القمة السعودية المصرية قُبَيْلَ انعقاد الدورة الجديدة للجنة العليا المصرية ـ السعودية المشتركة .

وأكد الدكتور عبد الأحد جمال الدين وكيل البرلمان المصري ان زيارة الرئيس مبارك لشقيقه خادم الحرمين الشريفين إنما تَعْكِسُ قي المَقام الأول عُمْق العلاقات المصرية السعودية سَواءً على المستوى القياديّ السياسيّ أو على المستوى الشعبي .

ووَصَفَ الدكتور محمد عبد اللاه رئيس لجنة العلاقات الخارجية في البرلمان المصري هذه الزيارة بأنها زيارة تخدم القضايا العربية الأساسيّة وفي مُقَدِّمَتها الخطوات الهامّة التي ستتّخذ على صعيد دول إعلان دمشق في مُخْتَلِف جوانبها السياسية والاقتصادية والأَمْنيّة .

al-Sharq al-Awasaṭ, 3 October 1991

3.4.2 Written/Oral Exercise

1. Listen to the following passages, which will each be read aloud twice at dictation speed by the teacher. As you listen, write down each passage in Arabic and translate it immediately into English.
2. Compare your versions of the passages with those below. Translate them into English orally, identifying and discussing any points of difficulty.

١ـ دعا مجلس الشُّورَى في الجمهورية العربية اليمنية قيادتَيْ شَطْرَي اليمن الى اتخاذ خطوة جادّة وعملية نَحْوَ تحقيق هدف الوطن اليمني في وَحْدَته . وجاءت هذه الدعوة في بيان أصدره المجلس عقب جَلْسَة خاصة عقدها أمس للاستماع الى ايضاحات قدمها وزير شؤون الوحْدة بالجمهورية العربية اليمنية حول سَيْر الجهود الرامية لتحقيق وحدة شطري اليمن .

٢ـ وجّه الرئيس حسني مبارك رسالة الى مؤتمر "قمة الطُّفولة" التي تبدأ اجتماعاتها بالأمم المتحدة اليوم ، والتي يشترك فيها

أكثر من ٧٥ ملكا ورئيس جمهورية ورئيس وزراء . وترأس السيدة سوزان مبارك وفد مصر في هذه القمة وتُلقي كلمتها أمام المؤتمر غدا . ويضم الوفد المصري السفير عمر موسى رئيس وفد مصر في الأمم المتحدة والدكتورة هُدى بدْران أمين عام المجلس القومي† للأمومة والطُفولة .

٣ـ اجتماع مشروع تَسْمِيَة القُرى الجديدة والشوارع والطرق الداخلية

مسقط ـ عقد صباح أمس الاجتماع الثالث عشر للجنة مشروع تسمية القرى الجديدة والشوارع والطرق الداخلية . وقد ترأس الاجتماع سعادة نايف بن عبيد السلامي وكيل وزارة البَلَديّات الإقليمية للشؤون الإدارية والمالية.

٤ـ وصل الى الاسكندرية أول من أمس ٤٨ من أعضاء "جَمْعيّة مُحبّي نابليون بونابرت" الفرنسية في بداية زيارة الى مصر تستغرق أسبوعين يجولون خلالها على المعالم الأثرية والتاريخية.

HOMEWORK

1. Compile a list of the new Arabic names of cities, countries and regions and adjectives of nationality/region used in Lessons 3.2–3.4.

2. Use each of the following words/phrases in a complete Arabic sentence of your own:

ـ على أَساس ... ـ مَوْقفٌ (من) ـ إداريٌّ ـ إقْليميٌّ
جَمْعيّةٌ ـ رَافَقَ ـ وَجَّهَ ـ هامٌّ ـ قُبَيْلَ ـ أوْ ... ـ سَواءٌ ...

3. Write four brief Arabic news stories of your own. Each should include the words/phrases given in one of the groups below.

---

†While the first title is given an (optional) feminine ending, the second is not. Note also the form taken by the *iḍāfah* in the second title.

(a)

اتّخذ خطوةً ـ سَيْرٌ ـ قِيادَةٌ ـ وَصَفَ + ه + بـ / بأنّه ـ بالغُ الأهمّيّة

(b)

ألْقى كلمةً (أمامَ) ـ شقيقٌ ـ مشروعٌ ـ أمْنٌ ـ مَجالٌ

(c)

عَكَسَ ـ في المَقام الأول ـ تَقارَبَ ـ حَقَّقَ ـ في مُقَدِّمَتِها

(d)

شَطْرٌ ـ رَبَطَ بين ـ علاقات الأُخُوّة ـ مَجهودٌ ـ نَظَراً لـ

UNIT 4

Vocabulary

In order to align its vocabulary and phraseology with those of the world press, Media Arabic coins numerous neologisms on a day-to-day basis. Many are too recent to have found their way into dictionaries, and many are ephemeral. This has two consequences for the learner.

First, the dictionary is of limited use in translation. When translating out of Arabic, look first at a word's context, and refer to your knowledge of currently fashionable English words and phrases to narrow down its meaning. When translating into Arabic, take the vocabulary you need from recently-published Arabic news reports on appropriate topics, rather than from a dictionary.

Second, when developing your vocabulary in specific areas, be prepared to discard old items and learn new ones on a short-term basis. Trends in English journalese may help to indicate which Arabic terms are likely to drop out of fashion quickly.

The ability to work out the meaning of unfamiliar or very recent coinages comes with practice. Initially at least, it will be found difficult to work them out by ear alone. Accordingly, this unit gives rather more space to reading and analysis than do the preceding units.

LESSON 4.1: FORMATION OF COINAGES

The following is a description of some of the methods by which coinages
are produced. These methods will be familiar from Modern Standard
Arabic, and examples have already been met in the course of Units 1–3.
(The terms employed in this description are not necessarily sanctioned by
technical usage, and the categorisations are not exhaustive. They are
designed as a rough framework to aid identification and assimilation of
new material.)

● **Transliteration/transcription**

The letters or sounds of a foreign word are written in Arabic characters.
Often Arabic word patterns are imposed on the borrowed word
(feminine singular marker, broken plural pattern, verb patterns, etc.)

Four points in particular should be noted when reading Media Arabic.
First, there are no firm rules for the length of vowels. Variant spellings
are found:

ديمقراطيّة or ديموقراطيّة

Second, place-names are usually rendered according to sound, not
according to their original spelling. Foreign place-names may enter
Arabic either through the original language:

بروكسل

جنيف

or via another language:

ألمانيا

النرويج

Third, regional differences of pronunciation may determine which letters
are used to represent sounds absent from Classical Arabic:

إنْكِليز   إنْجِليز

Regional differences may also affect syllabification:

أمْريكا   أمِيرْكا

Where suitable technology is available, fuller transliteration may be
attempted by forming new letters. For example:

ڤ for v

Finally, neologisms based on transliteration/transcription derive from a wide range of languages, and distortions sometimes occur. Some forms are easily confused with existing Arabic words or roots. For example:

كرْيم   French: *crème*; English: 'cream', as in 'face-cream'; unrelated to the Arabic root /k r m/

مُناوَرَة 'manoeuvre'; unrelated to the Arabic root /n w r/

- **Calque, or 'tracing'**

  Calque is a method of neologism-formation which tries exactly to translate a foreign word or phrase, using Arabic roots and Arabic syntax:

رَجُلُ أَعْمالٍ   French: *homme d'affaires* → businessman

مفاوضاتٌ متعدِّدةُ الأَطْرافِ   multilateral negotiations

ضَغَطَ (على)   to press down on (physically or figuratively)

ضُغوطٌ   pressures (e.g. political, psychological)

مارَسَ الضَّغْطَ / الضُّغوطَ على   to exercise/exert/put pressure on

In some instances, however, transferring a form of words from a foreign language to Arabic entails changes to normal Arabic syntax, most notably in the case of *mā idhā*. *Mā idhā* + conditional construction may replace *hal* in indirect questions, and is a translation of 'whether' interpreted as a vague conditional.

Compare سأله هل هناك احتمال لقاء بين الرئيسين

and سأله ما إذا كان هناك احتمال لقاء بين الرئيسين

Another instance of this phenomenon is the alteration of a verb's construction to bring it into line with that of a foreign-language counterpart. For example,

to suffer from   عَانَى من

is now very generally used in place of the grammatically correct *'ānā* + accusative.

● **Echoing**

'Echoing' is a loose description of the relationship between an Arabic formula and its foreign-language counterpart, where differences in wording or phrasing initially obscure the fact that the two formulae are identical:

مَصادِرُ اشْترطت عَدَمَ كَشْفِ هُوِيَّتِها

sources which have asked to remain anonymous

● **Aetiology**

Aetiology is a type of coinage which clarifies the content of the new term, explaining the 'reason' why it means what it does. This may be achieved by either of two methods.

First, in patterning, a new term is developed from an Arabic root, using word patterns with distinctive semantic connotations. This procedure is formally identical to the method by which the majority of Arabic words are produced; it differs from it when there is an underlying reference to a foreign term. For example:

هَاتِفٌ	(active participle of *hatafa*, 'to call') = تلفون	
غَوّاصة	submarine (noun) (from *ghāṣa*, 'to dive')	(intensive/ habitual
غَسّالة	washing-machine (from *ghasala*, 'to wash')	noun pattern)
تَعَدُّدِيّة	pluralism (form V *maṣdar* + abstract ending)	

Second, in *descriptive paraphrase*, the sequence noun + adjective is used to describe the object denoted by a foreign term:

satellite   قَمَرٌ صِناعيٌّ

Longer forms of descriptive paraphrase are also found:

anti-aircraft submarine   غوّاصة مُضادّة للطائرات

Note in this context a tendency in Arabic, as compared to English, to use self-explanatory rather than abbreviated or figurative terms. For example:

the media   وسائلُ الإعْلامِ

the press   الصُّحُفُ

The above examples are all fixed formulae, but descriptive paraphrases also occur as variable formulations, or as definitions rather than translations, as in the following examples, which refer to postnatal depression and sexual harassment:

ـ قد تُصاب المرأة بالحُزْن والوجوم بعد الولادة، ذلك العَرَضُ الشائعُ الى حَدٍّ أنه أصبح عاديا في كثير من المجتمعات .

ـ المرأة العاملة قد تعاني من تحرُّش الرجال بها.

- **Compounds**

Compound *adjectives* may be formed by:
amalgamation, the elements of the compound nevertheless being written separately. For example:

الشرق الأوسط the Middle East ← شرق أوسطيٌّ Middle Eastern

fusion, the elements of the compound being joined together:

رأس مال capital ← رأسماليٌّ capitalist

a combination of descriptive paraphrase and fusion, the elements of the compound being joined together, sometimes with the loss of one or more letters:

بَرٌّ land + water ← ماءٌ amphibious بَرْمائيٌّ

abbreviation:

الأُمَم المتحدة the UN ← أُمَميٌّ (pertaining to the) UN

juxtaposition or hyphenation:

العلاقات الصينية السوفياتية Sino-Soviet relations

المباحثات اللبنانية ـ الإسرائيلية talks between Lebanon and Israel

This category of adjectives forms a limited series in English, whereas in Arabic any two adjectives of nationality may be juxtaposed/hyphenated.

Compound *nouns* are simply *iḍāfah*s whose two elements continue to be written separately though the grammatical vowelling of the first may be slurred in pronunciation. For example:

reaction رَدُّ فِعْلٍ

- بوش يفتتح مؤتمر السلام : ردود(ُ) فِعْلِ أعضاء الوفود تُراوحُ بين التحفّظ والارْتياح

Plural forms of compound nouns vary. Either the first element (as in the above example), or both, may take the plural form. In some compounds, the second element is always in the plural. For example:

رِجالُ أعْمالٍ .pl رَجُلُ أعْمالٍ

Rarely, the elements of the compound are fused, and a broken plural pattern is applied to the whole:

رؤوسُ أموالٍ .pl رأسُ مالٍ

or

رساميلُ .pl رأسمال

Note a tendency, in the case of some titles, to treat noun + adjective sequences as compound nouns:

يضم الوفد المصري الدكتورة هُدى بدران أمين عام المجلس القومي للأمومة والطفولة

- **Semantic restriction**

    The semantic range of an existing word can be restricted and fixed in relation to a specific context. For example:

    اكْتَأَبَ to be dejected, morose, sad etc. →

    اكْتِئابُ (*maṣdar*) depression (clinical term)

Since there are no markers to show whether such a word is being used in its general or its restricted sense, coinages of this type are sometimes difficult to detect and interpret. In the following example, knowledge of the context (the passage is from a magazine article on 'coping with depression') enables the reader to identify the key words as clinical terms:

قد تكتئب المرأة وهي بنت عندما تتعرض لكل الضغوط الأُسرية،
وقد تكتئب عندما تتزوج، وبالطبْع تكتئب إذا طلقت . وقد تصاب
بالحزن والوجوم بعد الولادة ، وقد تكتئب ويكتئب معها زوجها إذا
لم تُنْجِب ، فتصاب بالإحْباط والضّيِق . والمرأة العاملة تشعر
بالاكتئاب نتيجةَ تحرّش الرجال بها .

The application of a word can also be restricted by the addition of a
marker. For example:

استقلاليّة ← استقلال

Compare

يعيش الشعب الجزائري تحت نِظام الحزب الواحد منذ الاستقلال

and

اعطت الحكومة مجالس إدارة الشركات التي تموّلها الاستقلالية
الكاملة عن الوزارات التابعة لها .

> Note that the distinction made in Arabic by the addition of
> such a marker may not always be reproducible in translation, as
> in the above example.
> Note that *al-wizārāt al-tābi'ah lahā* = 'the ministries in charge of
> (state-funded companies)'. For further discussion of the phrase
> *tābi' li-*, see Part II, page 122.

● **Additional remarks**

The same foreign term may give rise to more than one Arabic term:

طائرة مِحْوَريّة   =   طائرة عَموديّة   =   هليكوبتر

(transliteration + two different descriptive paraphrases)

Such duplication may occur when different languages are referred to in
coining a term:

Arabic word-pattern: 'the workforce'	العَمالة
cf. English: 'the workforce'	القُوَى العامِلة
cf. French: la main-d'œuvre	اليد العامِلة
cf. French: les années soixante	سنوات الستّينات

cf. English: 'the sixties' الستّينات / الستّينيّات

Increasingly characteristic of Media Arabic is the adoption or quotation of foreign metaphors and idioms:

ـ خطف الرئيس الأمريكي جورج بوش الأضْواءَ في الجلسة الافتتاحية لمؤتمر السلام في مدريد أمس .

ـ تصف مصادر مُقَرَّبَة من رئيس الوزراء الإسرائيلي الكلمة الافتتاحية للرئيس جورج بوش في مؤتمر السلام في مدريد بأنها "سَحابة ذات بِطانة فِضّيّة" .

Most are based on English models, as in the above examples, but some derive from French, as seems to be the case with the final phrase of the following passage:

إنه من المنتظر في سنوات التسعينات ان تُدْرِك القوى السياسية الإسلامية في مصر ان تأثيرها السياسي يرتبط الى حدّ كبير بتأكيد وتعميق الديموقراطية .

The stiff and padded style characteristic of most of the examples of Media Arabic studied so far may be relaxed under the influence of foreign models. This entails a move away from familiar 'frames' and 'fillings', a more dramatic presentation, and the adoption of a more graphic vocabulary:

في الوقت الذي أشْرَفت فيه دراما الرهائن† على آخر فصولها وصل الرهينة البريطاني السابق جاك مان (٧٧ عاما) الى بلاده أمس واستُقْبِل استقبالَ الأبْطال .

Resemblances between Arabic words/phrases and the foreign-language counterparts are not necessarily proof of borrowing. A familiar case in point is the Quranic *ra's māl*, 'capital'.

CLASSROOM PRACTICE

4.1.1 Written/ *Oral Exercise

1. Referring to the examples above, use each of the following words/ phrases in a complete Arabic sentence of your own:

ـ تَعَرَّضَ لِ ـ أُصيبَ بِ ـ مصادرُ اشترطت عَدَمَ كَشْفِ هويّتها ـ مصادرُ مُقَرَّبَةٌ من ـ راوَحَ بين ... و ...

†In the above sense of 'hostage', *rahīnah* is treated grammatically as masculine or feminine according to the gender of the person denoted. In the plural, it takes a plural adjective. This contrasts with the behaviour of *shakhṣiyyah* noted in Unit 2, Lesson 2.1.

2. Referring to the examples above, write an Arabic news story of your own using the following words/phrases in any order you wish:

رهينةٌ ـ عَرَضٌ شائعٌ ـ عَانى (من) ـ ضَغْطٌ ـ نَتيجَةَ

*3. Take it in turns to read your own stories aloud and to translate each other's stories orally.

4.1.2 Written/Oral Exercise

1. In writing, translate the words/phrases underlined in the following passages.

2. Read the passages aloud and translate them orally, explaining how you worked out the meaning of the words/phrases underlined.

١ـ في بيان مشترك صدر في طهران والدوحة طالبت ايران وقطر بإزالة الأسْلحة النووية وغيرها من أسلحة الدَّمار الشامل من مختلف أنحاءَ العالم .

٢ـ أفاد تقرير لمنظمة يهودية نُشرامس ان معاداة السامية عادت إلي الظهور في وسط أوروبا وشرقها بعد انهيار الشيوعية وصرح أحد مديري المؤتمر اليهودي العالمي بأنها "مسألة أثارت قَلَق اليهود في أنحاء العالم" . ووِرد في التقرير ان أحزابا سياسية عدة في بولندا و المجر ورومانيا تستخدم وَرَقَةَ معاداة السامية في صِراعها على السُّلْطة .

٣ـ ذكرت "جماعة السلام الأخضر" المُهْتَمَّة بـ حماية البيئة امس ان أمطارا سوداء تسقط على ايران. وقال خبير بشؤون البيئة تابع لـ "جماعة السلام الأخضر" ان ايران أصيبت بـ تلوّث بالغ ولكن من الصعب تحديد ما إذا كان النفط الخام الذي سبّب هذا التلوّث قد تسرّب أثناءَ حرب الخليج او الحرب العراقية ـ الايرانية .

٤ـ أعلنت شركة "شارب" اليابانية عن تطويـر اول **جهاز كمبيوتر**
شخصي بِحَجْم المفكّرة ذي **شاشة كريستالية ملوّنة** مساحتها
٤، ٨ إنش مربّع وسُمْكها ١٢ مليمترا. وقالت "شارب" ان الجهاز
الجديد **متوافق** مع أجهزة "أي ـ بي ـ إم" .

٥ـ لندن ـ رمى رجل بريطاني طفلته البالغة من العمر خمسة
أشهر في نهر **التيمز** حتى لا تعيش مع أمها التي كانت قد مُنحت
حق الحضانة.

4.1.3 Oral Exercise

Translate the following sentences into Arabic:

1. Anti-Semitism is reappearing all over the world.
2. The resurgence of anti-Semitism in both eastern and western Europe has alarmed Jews the world over.
3. Iran has called for the scrapping of nuclear arms and other weapons of mass destruction.
4. A report published yesterday says that working women often suffer from depression as a result of sexual harassment.
5. The board of directors has refused to finance the project.
6. Sources close to the vice-president say that his own political influence is closely linked to that of his wife on the First Lady.
7. The former hostages were given a hero's welcome when they arrived home yesterday.
8. It was the former hostage's wife who stole the limelight when the couple arrived in London yesterday.
9. Iran has suffered extensive pollution in the wake of the Gulf War.
10. A Japanese company has developed a new IBM-compatible personal computer the size of a teacup.

*4.1.4 Oral Exercise

Translate the following passage into Arabic, section by section:

What will be the future of the North African states in the twenty-first century? / Morocco is a kingdom, Algeria, Tunisia and Libya republics./ Libyans still live under one-party rule, but political pluralism has recently re-emerged in Tunisia. / It is difficult to say exactly what the influence

of the Islamic parties will be in the end. / At the moment, a power
struggle is taking place between the supporters of pluralism and those
who want a return to Islam. / All the North African countries are
suffering from severe economic problems, / and experts say that it is
these economic difficulties which have led to the emergence of Islamic
political parties in the region. / They consider the solution to Algeria's
present political problems.to be closely linked / to the finding of a lasting
solution to the economic problems which beset the Algerian people, and
from which they have suffered ever since independence in 1962.

HOMEWORK

1. Use each of the following words/phrases in a complete Arabic
   sentence of your own:

صَدَرَ ـ نَشَرَ ـ مَنَحَ ـ طَالَبَ + ه + بِ ـ سَبَّبَ ـ أَثَارَ ـ طَوَّرَ ـ
مَوَّلَ ـ تَابِعٌ لِ

2. Write three brief Arabic news stories of your own. Each should
   contain the words/phrases given in one of the groups below.

(a)

تَأْثِيرٌ ـ نِظامُ الحِزبِ الواحد ـ استقلالٌ ـ أَشْرَفَ على ـ تَعَدُّدِيَّةٌ

(b)

مجلسُ إِدارةٍ ـ جِهازٌ ـ (سنوات) التسعينات ـ تَحَفُّظٌ

(c)

طَلَّقَ ـ حقُّ الحضانةِ ـ اكْتِئَابٌ ـ إِحْباطٌ ـ ارْتِياحٌ

3. Written translation of 4.1.3 Oral Exercise.
*4. Written translation of 4.1.4 Oral Exercise.

REVISION

4.1.5 Oral Exercise

Translate the following sentences into Arabic:

1. The two prime ministers will review the latest regional developments, with particular reference to the resurgence of anti-Semitism.
2. A report published yesterday says that working women are often
   subject to sexual harassment and other pressures.
3. The Saudi Foreign Minister has called for increased efforts to rid the
   world of nuclear arms and other weapons of mass destruction.
4. His Iranian counterpart has welcomed his proposals and called for
   joint Islamic action in this area.

5. The UN envoy has called on regional bodies to cooperate in finding a just and lasting solution.
6. Arab diplomatic circles have described a report published recently by a Jewish organisation as untrustworthy.
7. The company's director is to announce his resignation, after refusing to finance a project which he described as likely to lead to extensive pollution.
8. Environmental experts say that Iran has suffered extensive pollution, caused by leakages of crude oil during the Gulf War.
9. The company is currently working on the development of a notebook-sized IBM-compatible personal computer.
10. The woman was granted custody of her five-year-old daughter after her father threw her into the Thames.

*4.1.6 Oral Exercise

Translate the following sentences into Arabic:

1. The French and German leadership will review local and regional developments, with particular reference to the re-emergence of anti-Semitism in both eastern and western Europe.
2. A report published recently says that working women are subject to a variety of pressures, notably sexual harassment and family pressure.
3. The French Foreign Ministry spokesman clarified his government's attitude towards nuclear arms, and his Kuwaiti counterpart called for increased efforts to rid the world of weapons of mass destruction.
4. An Iranian government spokesperson has welcomed proposals to eliminate nuclear weapons, and has called on Arab and Islamic leaders to cooperate in this sphere in view of its special importance.
5. At a press conference yesterday, the UN envoy reviewed the progress of the unilateral talks and called for increased cooperation from regional bodies, particularly the Gulf Cooperation Council, in finding a just and lasting solution.
6. Arab diplomatic circles describe the talks as successful, and dismiss a report by Jewish organisations, which calls the outcome of the talks 'negative', as untrustworthy.
7. The organisation's executive committee has refused to finance this and other projects, and has called on the directors to resign.
8. Interviewed by *The Times*, an environmental expert has said that it is difficult to say for sure whether crude oil spilt during the Gulf War has caused the extensive pollution suffered by Iran during the past year.
9. The Regional Committee for the Naming of New Villages and Streets is to use an IBM-compatible computer developed by a Japanese company.

10. The man, who had earlier thrown his daughter in the Thames, was said to have been suffering from anxiety and depression. The mother expressed her relief on learning that she had been granted custody of the child.

4.1.7 Written Exercise

Listen to sentences from either/both 4.1.5 and 4.1.6 being read aloud at dictation speed by the teacher. As you listen, write an Arabic translation of the sentences.

LESSON 4.2: COINAGES IN POLITICS

This lesson continues the work on coinages done in the previous lesson. The journalistic formulae reviewed in Units 1–3 relate to political figures and politics in the broad sense; the material in this lesson gives examples of the types of neologism that you may expect to encounter in such contexts.

CLASSROOM PRACTICE

4.2.1 Written/Oral Exercise

The following passages contain old and new coinages relating to politics.
1. In writing, translate into English the words/phrases underlined.
2. Read the passages aloud and translate them orally, explaining how you worked out the meaning of the words/phrases underlined.

١ـ أعلنت وكالة الأنباء اليوغوسلافية أمس ان الحكومة اليوغوسلافية قررت <u>إعادة علاقاتها الدبلوماسية مع</u> إسرائيل. وكانت يوغوسلافية <u>قطعت علاقاتها الدبلوماسية</u> مع إسرائيل خلال حرب يونيو ١٩٦٧ .

٢ـ <u>طَغَى</u> الخطاب الذي ألقاه الرئيس جورج بوش امس في مدريد <u>على</u> جلسة افتتاح مؤتمر السلام الذي تشارك فيه <u>أطراف النِّزاع الشرق الأوسطي</u> بعدما حدّد أهداف هذا المؤتمر بالوصول الى "معاهدات سلام" بين إسرائيل وكل من سورية والاردن ولبنان "وليس <u>مُجَرَّد</u> إنهاء حال الحرب" إضافةً الى <u>التطبيع الكامل للعلاقات بين</u> دول المنطقة . وأثار الخطاب ردود <u>فعل مُتَفاوتَة</u> بين أعضاء الوفود راوحت بين التحفظ السوري و <u>الارتياح الحَذِر</u> للوفدين الفلسطيني والإسرائيلي، في حين أظهر الوفد الأردني <u>تَفاؤُلاً حَذِرا</u> .

٣ـ أعربت لجنة العلاقات الخارجية في البرلمان المصري عن أملها في نجاح مؤتمر السلام في التوصّل الى   تَسْوِيَة سِلْمِية متوازنة وعادلة للصراع العربي ـ الإسرائيلي تكفل للشعب الفلسطيني ممارسة حقوقه المشروعة في الحرية   و تقرير المصير .

٤ـ أوْضح المستشار السياسي للعاهل الأردني ان المفاوضات ستكون عميقة ومعقَّدة وقال انه ستتم   تسوية المَطالِب الأردنية والسورية واللبنانية خلال السنة الأولى من المفاوضات في حين ستستغرق تسوية المطالب الفلسطينية ٤ـ٥ سنوات ، مؤكدا انه سيتم إعطاء السُّكّان العرب من أهالي القدس الشرقية حق المشاركة في المفاوضات الخاصّة بتحقيق حُكْم ذاتي للفلسطينيين في الضِّفَّة والقِطاع .

٥ـ اقترح وزير الدولة النمسوي للشؤون الخارجية إنشاء "سوق عربية مُشْتَرَكة" في الشرق الأوسط تضم إسرائيل بِصِفَة "عضو مشارك" او دائم وقال ان تحقيق أمن وسلام دائمين في المنطقة يتم على أساس تحقيق تكامل اقتصادي بين بلدان المنطقة.

٦ـ كازخستان أسرع الجمهوريات السوفياتية السابقة نحو تطبيق اقتصاد السوق

بدأت جمهوريات آسيا الوسطى تشكيل اتحاد جديد والتنسيق بين سياساتها الاقتصادية وذلك بعد ان أصبح تفكّك الاتحاد السوفياتي أمراً واقعا .

4.2.2 *Oral Exercise*

Translate the following sentences into Arabic:

1. Anti-Semitism has begun to resurface in Europe as a result of the break-up of the Soviet Union.
2. One of the results of the collapse of the Soviet regime has been the ending of one-party rule and the re-emergence of political pluralism in eastern Europe.
3. The collapse of communism has led to the normalisation of Russia's relations with the West.
4. Economic integration will be one of the goals of the former Soviet republics.
5. Reactions to the president's opening speech varied, ranging from relief to cautious optimism.
6. Self-determination is considered a basic human right.
7. In her speech yesterday, the Palestinian spokeswoman demanded autonomy for Palestinians in the Gaza Strip and West Bank.
8. Sources close to King Hassan of Morocco say that he is about to invite Algeria and Tunisia to form a North African common market.
9. A number of UN organisations have been working to bring about a settlement of the conflict.
10. King Hussein's political adviser has said that it will take a year to satisfy Jordanian demands.

4.2.3 Oral Exercise

Translate the following passage into Arabic, section by section:

The opening session of the conference was dominated by the speech made by the Palestinian representative. / She said that negotiations aimed at securing a just, fair and lasting settlement would be complex, / and that the Arab population of East Jerusalem must be involved in any talks with Israel / concerning Palestinian autonomy in the West Bank and Gaza Strip. / She invited the Arab parties to the Middle East conflict to coordinate their efforts. / The political adviser to King Hussein of Jordan also made a speech in which he said that the aim of the current talks / was not simply to end the state of war existing in the region / but a complete normalisation of relations and restoration of diplomatic links between the parties to the conflict. / He said that any settlement must guarantee the Palestinians' right to self-determination / and should not be influenced by pressures brought to bear by Jewish bodies outside Israel.

4.2.4 Written Exercise

1. Listen to the following sentence, which will be read aloud twice at dictation speed by the teacher. Write down the words/phrases stressed (underlined in the text) in Arabic and translate them into English.

2. Compare your notes with the text below, and translate the whole sentence into English.

جاء في تقرير ان الصين تساهم في بناء مُفاعل للأبحاث النووية

في ايران في اطار برنامج ايراني سِرّي لـ تصنيع أسلحة نووية .

HOMEWORK

1. Translate 4.2.1 Written Exercise into idiomatic English.
2. Written translation of 4.2.2 Oral Exercise.
*3. Written translation of 4.2.3 Oral Exercise.
4. Use each of the following words/phrases in a complete Arabic sentence of your own:

مُجَرَّدٌ ... ـ مُعَقَّدٌ ـ التنْسيقُ بين ـ طَغَى على ـ خاصٌّ بـ ـ
عُضْوٌ مُشاركٌ ـ عُضْوٌ دائمٌ ـ كَفَلَ ـ إعادةُ العلاقات
الدبلوماسية مع ـ ساهَمَ في

5. Write an Arabic news story of your own using the following words/ phrases in any order you wish:

مُفاعلٌ ـ سِرّيٌّ ـ أمرٌ واقعٌ ـ تفاؤُلٌ حَذِرٌ ـ مُسْتَشارٌ

LESSON 4.3: NEW VOCABULARY: USING NEWSPAPERS AS A SOURCE

When using Arabic newspapers as a source of vocabulary, be careful to identify the construction used with each word as well as its meaning.

CLASSROOM PRACTICE

4.3.1 Written Exercise

The following passages from political news items contain 'frames' which, in contrast to the mainly neutral synonyms of *qāla* reviewed so far, express positive or negative attitudes.

1. Read the passages silently. Do not translate them.
2. Identify in the passages the Arabic equivalents of the English words/ phrases below, and use each in a complete Arabic sentence of your own.

to refuse - threat – condemnation – to deny – to regard as unlikely – to criticise

١ـ انتقدت ايران الكويت لتوقيعها اتفاقية عسكرية مع الولايات المتحدة .

٢ـ نفت الصين تقارير من الولايات المتحدة جاء فيها ان الصين تساهم في بناء مفاعل للأبحاث النووية في ايران في اطار برنامج ايراني سري لتصنيع أسلحة نووية .

٣ـ نفى وزير خارجية جنوب افريقيا امس في القدس المحتلة وجود أي تعاون نووي بين بريتوريا وإسرائيل .

٤ـ أكد إعلان أصدرته القمة الإسلامية السادسة إدانة استخدام القوة والتهديد باستخدامها ضدّ وحدة أراضي أي دولة أو ضدِّ استقلالها السياسي .

٥ـ استبعد وزير الخارجية المصري ان يرفض الفلسطينيون المشاركة في مؤتمر السلام .

4.3.2 Oral Exercise

Translate the following sentences into Arabic:

1. The Palestinian delegation has refused to take part in multilateral talks.
2. The leader of the Palestinian delegation thought it unlikely that it would take part in the conference.
3. The leader of the Palestinian delegation has criticised what she called Israel's negative stance.
4. The leader of the Palestinian delegation said that their own attitude would always be positive, but dismissed what she called 'the negative attitude held by others'.
5. The Israeli prime minister has denied the existence of any military agreement between his government and the government of South Africa.
6. The new president said that any threat to use force against the government could lead to a very serious situation.
7. The king called for the cooperation of all Arab leaders in condemning the use of force.
8. Western leaders have condemned the use of force against Lebanon's territorial integrity.
9. When questioned by reporters, the Scottish Secretary said the government was unlikely to finance the scheme.
10. Referring to the existence of a nuclear reactor in Iraq, the American president said that the nuclear threat could only be ended by the total elimination of weapons of mass destruction.

*4.3.3 Oral Exercise

Translate the following passage into Arabic, section by section:

In a newspaper interview today, the leader of the Socialist party described his party's programme. / He condemned the government's fiscal policy / and said that it would lead to economic crisis. / He dismissed a government report published yesterday / which said that his party was financed by Libya, / and denied the existence of any link between his party and the Libyan government. / He added that his party condemned the use of force and the threat of force, / and criticised the government for using force against opposition parties. / He denied that there was a power struggle in the party between himself and the deputy leader, / and invited the prime minister to take part with him in a television interview to debate their parties' respective policies.

4.3.4 Written/ *Oral Exercise

The following passages from political news items contain miscellaneous vocabulary.

1. Read the passages silently. Do not translate them.
2. Use the vocabulary that they contain to write three brief Arabic news stories of your own. Each should include translations of the words/phrases given in one of groups (a)–(c) below.
*3. Take it in turns to read your own stories aloud and to translate each other's stories orally.

(a) to criticise – to warn (of) – dissolution/to dissolve – possibility
(b) to endorse a resolution – the international community – especially – to praise – mission – (UN) Security Council – to condemn
(c) again – separate (adjective) (negotiations, etc.) – to comment on – team – to rule out – – round (of talks, etc.)

١۔ رفض وزير الخارجية الصيني التعليق على تقارير من الولايات المتحدة جاء فيها ان الصين تساهم في بناء مفاعل للأبحاث النووية في ايران في اطار برنامج ايراني سري لتصنيع اسلحة نووية .

٢۔ لم يستبعد وزير الداخلية الجزائري إمكانية اتخاذ قرار بحلّ الجبهة الإسلامية للإنقاذ .

٣۔ حذّر عدد من الرؤساء الاوروبيين من النتائج المحتملة لتفكك الاتحاد السوفياتي .

٤۔ مجلس الأمن يُدين اسرائيل مجددا
وافقت الولايات المتحدة للمرة الثانية خلال ١٢ يوما على قرار لمجلس الامن يندد برفض الحكومة الاسرائيلية استقبال بَعْثة الامين العام للامم المتحدة الى الاراضي المحتلة .

٥۔ في الوقت الذي تبدأ فيه الجولة الثانية من المفاوضات الثنائية المنفردة بين الاطراف العربية والطواقم الاسرائيلية، أشاد الامين العام لمنظمة المؤتمر الاسلامي بـ "الجهود التي بذلها المجتمع الدولي خصوصا الولايات المتحدة" .

*4.3.5 Oral Exercise .

Translate the following sentences into Arabic:

1. The second round of negotiations opened yesterday.
2. The UN Secretary-General has praised the international community for its efforts to bring about peace in the Middle East.
3. The international community will condemn any threat to Israel's territorial integrity.
4. The Israeli team refuses to take part in separate negotiations with a Palestinian delegation.
5. The Israeli prime minister has again ruled out any possibility of separate negotiations with PLO representatives.
6. The USA is expected to endorse a UN resolution calling on Israel to receive the Secretary-General's mission to the Occupied Territories.
7. Arab leaders have renewed their call to the Security Council to condemn Israel's refusal to receive the Secretary-General's mission to the Occupied Territories.
8. The president has threatened to dissolve all opposition parties.
9. The president yesterday refused to comment on his threat to dissolve opposition parties.
10. The president has refused to comment on his threat, reported in yesterday's press, to dissolve all opposition parties, and has criticised opposition leaders for refusing to back government policy.

*4.3.6 Oral Exercise

Translate the following passage into Arabic, section by section:

A Foreign Office spokesman, commenting on reports from East Jerusalem, said / that the government condemned the use of force, and would call on Israel's prime minister / to receive the UN Secretary-General's mission to the Occupied Territories. / He said that Britain endorsed the Security Council resolution condemning Israel, / and noted the refusal of the Israeli team to negotiate separately with the Palestinian delegation. / Turning to other matters, he said that the government was alarmed by the Algerian government's threat to dissolve the opposition Islamic Salvation Front, / and expressed relief that the Algerian prime minister had not yet taken a decision on this matter, / and cautious optimism that he would take positive steps to restore democracy and pluralism. / He described western reactions to the situation in Algeria / as veering between concern and alarm.

4.3.7 Written Exercise

Listen to the following passage, which will be read aloud twice by the teacher, and which contains the Arabic equivalents of the English words/phrases listed below.

1. Identify and write down the corresponding Arabic terms.
2. Listen again to the passage being read aloud at dictation speed. As you listen, write an English translation of the passage.

principle – threat to peace and security – member state – continuing to/the continuation of – repudiation

أكد إعلان أصدرته القمة الإسلامية السادسة رفض وإدانة السياسات التي تدعم إسرائيل في مواصلة احتلال الأراضي العربية . وأكد الإعلان مبدأ الامتناع عن استخدام القوة والتهديد باستخدامها ضد وحدة أراضي أي دولة أو ضد استقلالها السياسي . واعتبر الإعلان أي تهديد لأمن أية دولة عضو تهديدا للسلم والأمن الدوليين .

4.3.8 Written Exercise

Repeat the above exercise, using the English words/phrases and the Arabic passage below:

principal – to follow (sthg.) with concern – supporter – to show/display – to constitute

يتابع المغاربة بالمزيد من الاهتمام تطورات الوضع في الجزائر على الرغم من ان المغاربة أبدوا في السابق ارتياحا كبيرا الى انهيار جبهة التحرير الوطني الجزائري التي شكّلت في رأيهم المساند الرئيسي لجبهة "بوليساريو" .

HOMEWORK

1. Compile a list of the new Arabic names of countries and places and adjectives of nationality used in Unit 4.
2. Translate 4.3.1 Written Exercise, sentences 1–5, into idiomatic English.
3. Written translation of 4.3.2 Oral Exercise and/or 4.3.5 Oral Exercise.
*4. Written translation of 4.3.3 Oral Exercise and/or 4.3.6 Oral Exercise.

5. Translate 4.3.4 Written Exercise, sentences 1–5, into idiomatic English.

6. Use each of the following words/phrases in a complete Arabic sentence of your own:

وَاصَلَ ـ تَابَعَ ـ اِحْتَلَّ ـ مَبْدَأً ـ اِمْتَنَعَ عن

*7. Identify the brands and products in the following slogans, which are typical of newspaper advertisements:

ـ إيميديا الجديد كريم لصبغ الشعر والعناية به

ـ كونيكا الناسخة الملونة لألوان طبيعية

ـ روثمان لايتس الجديد . النكهة التي اشتهرت في جميع انحاء العالم ... لك الآن بمذاق أخف

ـ ٧٥ عاما من النجاح : بوينغ الرائدة في تقنية صناعة الطيران

Newspaper Material –
Format and Style

GENERAL REMARKS

This unit sets the features of Media Arabic so far studied within the context of general features of the Arab press. It aims to develop a sense of the different formats and styles of writing that a newspaper reader can expect to encounter, and consists chiefly of reading and writing exercises. However, the first three items (all news reports) show no stylistic divergence from material already encountered, and should be treated as an opportunity for revision and for assessing progress to date.

The Arabic-language daily press falls into two main groups: the *internationals*, which are printed and distributed simultaneously in Europe, the Middle East and, usually, the USA (and, in some cases, Japan); and the *national dailies*, many of which are increasingly available overseas. The following internationals are among those with head offices in London, which has become an important centre of Arabic-language publishing: *al-Ahrām* (international edition of the semi-official Egyptian daily); *al-'Arab* (independent); *al-Ḥayāh* (Lebanese-owned, independent); *al-Quds al-'Arabī* (independent); *Ṣawt al-Kuwayt* (international edition); *al-Sharq al-Awsaṭ* (Saudi-owned).

A unified system of transliteration for Arabic titles has been adopted here and throughout this book. The systems actually employed by individual newspapers vary widely.

The internationals and the quality nationals are broadsheets. With the exception of *al-Ahrām*, they are produced technically to a high standard; colour printing may be used, and some papers have weekend reviews or colour supplements.

The nationality and/or political leanings of the international press may be reflected in their news coverage and sometimes in their style; *al-Ahrām*, for example, has an unmistakably Egyptian and pro-government slant; the Lebanese *al-Ḥayāh* and the Saudi *al-Sharq al-Awsaṭ* give particular prominence to Lebanese and Saudi news respectively. Such differences are of course still more marked in the national press, where the bulk of news may concern purely local affairs and where party loyalty or a sectarian stance may be openly advertised (for example, the Lebanese *al-Ḥadīth* is a Maronite paper; the Syrian *Tishrīn* is the mouthpiece of the ruling Ba'ath party; the Egyptian *al-Wafd* is published by the Wafd party and the Moroccan *al-Ittiḥād al-Ishtirākī* by the opposition al-Ittiḥād al-Ishtirākī li'l-Quwwāt al-Sha'biyyah party).

Nevertheless, there is a growing element of uniformity to be observed in both the international press and the quality national dailies in terms of both appearance and coverage; this can be attributed to the use of a common printing technology and common Arab and international news sources. (Some international papers also carry items translated directly from western papers; for example, *al-Ḥayāh*'s business pages include articles from the *Financial Times*). In addition, the stylistic gap between the leading papers appears to be narrowing: for example, the writing in *al-Ḥayāh* was, until recently, generally considered to be livelier and more sophisticated than that in *al-Sharq al-Awsaṭ* , but in the course of 1992 the latter's house style has begun to grow noticeably closer to that of its Lebanese competitor. While the basic style of Arabic journalese – written or broadcast – remains that illustrated by the items in this book, it is reasonable, in view of such developments, to anticipate that Media Arabic will become increasingly complex over the next few years.

The degree of independence existing in a local press, and the variety of viewpoints catered for, are not necessarily determined by the size of a country's population or the length of time for which journalism has existed there. Lebanon has a long-established and diverse independent press; Egypt, also with a long-standing tradition of journalism, has rather less diversity and press freedom; Kuwait and the Emirates, latecomers to journalism and with small populations, have a relatively large number of quality independent papers.

In connection with press freedom or the lack of it, the existence should be noted of an *overseas Arabic press*, much of it devoted to pro- or anti-government propaganda or polemic. It includes papers such as the Tehran-based *Kayhān al-'Arabī* , a mouthpiece of the Iranian government, and numerous weekly or occasional broadsheets or news-sheets, such as the Paris-based satirical *al-Muḥarrir* or the London-based Iraqi opposition weekly *Dār al-Salām*.

There appear to be no comprehensive, country-by-country surveys of the above type of publication; but, for fuller information on the officially-registered Arab press and media (whether Arabic or foreign-language), the following works should be consulted:

The Middle East and North Africa (London: Europa Publications; annually since 1948): its country-by-country surveys include listings of officially-registered local Arabic and foreign-language dailies, periodicals and radio and TV stations; details are also given of national press agencies.

William A. Rugh, *The Arab Press: News Media and Political Process in the Arab World*, second edition (Syracuse, New York: Syracuse University Press, 1987), is the standard textbook on the subject. It begins with a general survey of the Arab news media as institutions, discusses the economic, cultural and political factors that have shaped them, and goes on to describe contemporary national presses in detail in terms of their role in national political life. It includes substantial information on press ownership, control and censorship, as well as on foreign news sources used by the Arab press; it should be noted, however, that the international press has expanded greatly since the book appeared. There is also a brief chapter on radio and TV.

Douglas A. Boyd, *Broadcasting in the Arab World: A Survey of Radio and Television in the Middle East* (Philadelphia, Pennsylvania: Temple University Press, 1982) is the standard textbook for the broadcast media. A brief general introduction is followed by a thorough country-by-country survey and there are valuable sections on international broadcasting (to and from the Arab world, and including the BBC and Voice of America) and on clandestine broadcasting. (Further information on clandestine radio stations can occasionally be gleaned from specialist radio magazines.)

LESSON 5.1: TYPES OF MATERIAL

Excluding miscellaneous items (letters to the editor, advertisements, cartoons, funeral notices, etc.), newspaper material falls into five main categories, each of which has some special features of its own (length, format, syntax, vocabulary). These categories are: *news reports; investigative features; interviews; editorials/comment columns;* and *specialist articles* (finance and business; sport, culture; religion). Examples of each main category are given below, and should be skimmed through (and not translated unless otherwise indicated) with the aim of gaining a general impression of the style typical of each.

● **News reports**

A typical small news item will consist entirely of stereotyped 'frames' and 'fillings':

اتصال للامير عبد الله
بالعاهل المغربي

الرياض ـ واس: أجرى الأمير عبد الله
بن عبد العزيز ولي العهد ونائب رئيس
مجلس الوزراء ورئيس الحرس الوطني
السعودي اتصالا هاتفيا مساء امس الاول
بالملك الحسن الثاني ملك المملكة
المغربية.
وتم في الاتصال استعراض الاوضاع
الراهنة في ضوء المستجدات على
الصعيدين العربي والدولي وكل ما يخدم
قضايا الامتين العربية والاسلامية.

al-Sharq al-Awasaṭ, 14 October 1991

The same format is often applied to longer articles:

الأمير عبد الله يجري سلسلة لقاءات مع قادة الدول ورؤساء الوفود الإسلامية

دكار ـ واس: أجرى الأمير عبد الله بن عبد العزيز ولي العهد ونائب رئيس مجلس الوزراء ورئيس الحرس الوطني السعودي سلسلة جديدة من اللقاءات مع قادة الدول ورؤساء الوفود الاسلامية الى قمة دكار.

فقد استقبل الرئيس السنغالي عبده ضيوف رئيس مؤتمر القمة الاسلامية السادس في مكتبه بمقر المؤتمر ليلة أمس الأمير عبد الله.

وجرى خلال اللقاءات تبادل الاحاديث الودية والعلاقات الثنائية بين البلدين كما جرى بحث أهم القضايا المطروحة على جدول أعمال مؤتمر القمة الاسلامية.

وحضر المقابلة وزير المالية والاقتصاد الوطني السيد محمد أبا الخيل ووزير العمل والشؤون الاجتماعية السيد محمد علي الفايز وسفير السعودية في دكار السيد عبد الله الطبيشي.

وحضرها من الجانب السنغالي السيد مصطفى سيسي مستشار الرئيس السنغالي للشؤون الدينية والسياسية والسيد عثمان تنورجين رئيس ديوان رئاسة

الجمهورية ووزير الخارجية السيد دي بوكا.

واستقبل الأمير عبد الله بن عبد العزيز بمكتبه في مقر المؤتمر رئيس جمهورية سيراليون الدكتور جوزيف سعيدو مومو.

كما استقبل ولي العهد بمكتبه في مقر مؤتمر القمة داود جاوارا رئيس جمهورية جامبيا.

واستقبل الأمير عبد الله بن عبد العزيز رئيس حكومة انغانستان المؤقتة صبغة الله مجددي.

وحضر المقابلة وزير خارجية حكومة افغانستان المؤقتة برهان الدين رباني.

واستقبل الأمير عبد الله بن عبد العزيز رئيس وزراء النيجر شيخ أحمد.

كما استقبل ولي العهد في مكتبه بمقر المؤتمر نائب رئيس وزراء ماليزيا كافا بابا.

واستقبل الأمير عبد الله بن عبد العزيز ولي العهد ونائب رئيس مجلس الوزراء ورئيس الحرس الوطني في مكتبه بمقر المؤتمر وزير خارجية الجزائر الأخضر الابراهيمي.

al-Sharq al-Awasaṭ, 12 December 1991

Conventional 'frames' may be abandoned and a narrative or analytical style closer to that of ordinary Modern Standard Arabic adopted:

■ تواجه عملية تشكيل الحكومة الكويتية الجديدة بعض المصاعب والمشاكل التي قد تؤدي الى تاخير هذا التشكيل اياماً اخرى.

وأول هذه المشاكل اصرار المعارضة الكويتية على بعض الشروط من اجل المشاركة في هذه الحكومة.

وعلى رغم ان ولي العهد رئيس الحكومة المكلف الشيخ سعد العبدالله يحبذ تحقيق مشاركة شعبية من

جميع الفعاليات والقوى السياسية والاقتصادية والاجتماعية الا انه ابلغ الى الذين اجتمع بهم ان الحكم يرفض اي شروط من احد للمشاركة في الحكومة وان الشرط الاساسي الذي تضعه القوى السياسية للمشاركة، وهو اعلان موعد محدد لا يتجاوز ستة اشهر لاجراء انتخابات نيابية في الكويت، هو بيد الامير الشيخ جابر الاحمد.

al-Ḥayāh, 5 April 1991

5.1.1 Written Exercise

Read the three passages above silently.

1. Use each of the following words/phrases from the first passage in a complete Arabic sentence of your own:

أُمَّةٌ ـ ... فِي ضَوْءِ ـ راهِنٌ ـ بِ ـ أَجْرى اتّصالاً هاتفيّاً

2. In the second passage, find the Arabic terms corresponding to the following English words/phrases:

series – conference headquarters – agenda – provisional/interim government

3. In the third passage, find the Arabic terms corresponding to the English words/phrases given below, and use each in a complete Arabic sentence of your own:

to face – insistence (upon)/to insist upon – condition – to approve – parliamentary elections

5.1.2 Oral Exercise

Read the second passage aloud and translate it into English paragraph by paragraph.·

5.1.3 Written Exercise

Listen to the first passage, which will be read aloud at dictation speed by the teacher. As you listen, write a translation of the passage in idiomatic English.

5.1.4 Written Exercise

Summarise the third passage in English.

● **Investigative features**
Investigative features adopt an even freer format than news items of type in the third passage above. The devices used to highlight the human-interest element of stories are reminiscent both of western journalism and of Arabic broadcast news features. Here are the first five paragraphs of a typical feature:

□ غرفة عمليات بالخارجية لتأمين عودة وسلامة المصريين :

« وثيقة طريق » ومساعدة مالية لكل مصرى عائد للوطن

كيف تبدو الصورة داخل المكتب الذى خصصته وزارة الخارجية المصرية لتلقى طلبات المواطنين للاتصال بابنائهم وعائلاتهم العاملين داخل الكويت والذين حالت الظروف دون خروجهم بعد اغلاق الحدود وقطع الاتصالات التليفونية وهل استطاع العاملون بالمكتب تحقيق الاطمئنان على احوال المصريين هناك .. وماذا تقول البرقيات القادمة من السفارة المصرية فى الكويت بعد ان بدأت المحاولات فى الاتصال بالمصريين والاطمئنان على احوالهم .. وماذا اعدت الخارجية المصرية من وسائل واتصالات حتى تضمن عودتهم سالمين الى أرض الوطن ؟

أكد الدكتور عصمت عبد المجيد نائب رئيس الوزراء وزير الخارجية ان مصر تتابع باهتمام بالغ حالة المواطنين المصريين فى الكويت والعراق ، وان مصر بكل طاقتها تبذل جهدا كبيرا فى حماية امن المواطنين المصريين هناك .

ومازالت غرفة العمليات المشكلة فى وزارة الخارجية برئاسة السفير حسان العبادى مساعد الوزير تتابع مع السفارة المصرية فى الكويت اوضاع المصريين .

الاف من الطلبات تتلقاها وزارة الخارجية يوميا من اسر المصريين العاملين بالكويت للاطمئنان على ارواحهم وسلامتهم وسط الدوامة التى تلف الخليج بموجات من الرعب والغموض . والصورة من داخل ادارة القنصليات بالوزارة حيث تجمع مئات المواطنين وقد انتابهم القلق والتوتر الشديدان إزاء مايتلقونه يوميا من انباء غامضة عن اوضاع ابنائهم وعائلاتهم العاملين فوق أرض الكويت . وزير الخارجية عصمت عبد المجيد يستقبل عشرات منهم ويهدى من روعهم مؤكدا ان الحكومة المصرية تبذل جهدها للاطمئنان اليومى على ابنائها فى الكويت وتيسير انتقالهم الى القاهرة والسفير شريف المراغى مدير ادارة القنصليات يرفع حالة الطوارىء بالادارة ويمد ساعات العمل حتى وقت متأخر لمواجهة الاف الطلبات المقدمة للادارة يوميا .

al-Ahrām, 12 August 1990

● **Interviews**

Similarly, newspaper interviews attempt to reproduce the features of broadcast interviews. The following is an extract from a half-page interview with an Albanian Muslim leader. Three paragraphs of introductory matter have been omitted and the interview itself has been cut. Note the use of bold print.

● كيف وجدتم وضع المسلمين الالبان بعد السنوات الطويلة من الحكم الشيوعي؟

ـ وضع المسلمين في البانيا بعد السنوات الطويلة من الحكم الشيوعي وضع سيئ بل هو أسوأ وضع للمسلمين رأيته في انحاء العالم كله ـ وقد زرت العالم كله ـ والمراد بذلك وضعهم من الناحية الدينية. ففي خلال الحكم الشيوعي اغلقت جميع المساجد دون استثناء وحطمت مساجد كثيرة وسويت بالارض حتى لم يبق لها أثر، وصودرت مساجد أخرى بعد ان هدمت مناراتها التي هي شعار اسلامي ظاهر، ثم استعملت المساجد مخازن أو معامل أو مساكن للشبيبة الشيوعية وأمثالها، وحرم على الناس ان يؤدوا شعيرة من شعائر الاسلام سواء أكان ذلك سراً أم علناً، فكانوا يسلطون حتى تلاميـذ المدارس على أهاليـهم ليـعرفوا مـاذا يقولون في البيت؟ فاذا كانوا يصلون سراً أو حتى يتلفظون بالشـهادتين في بيوتهم عوقبوا عقاباً مريراً!

وقـد تجـولنا في انحـاء البلاد في صحبـة مفتي البـانيا الشيخ حافظ صبـري كـوتشـي رئيس الجـمـعـيـة الاسلامية، فزرنا المدن والقرى والأرياف واطلعنا على اشلاء بعض المساجد كما اطلعنا على أماكن، كانت مسـاجد، لم يبق لها من أثر إلا في ذاكرة بعض كبار السن من المسلمين، ورأينا مع الأسف الشديد ان ناشئة المسلمين لا يحسنون حتى التلفظ بالشـهادتين فـلا يستطيع الشـاب ان يعـرف لفظ «لا إله إلا الله محمد رسول الله».

ولقـد تملكنا العـجب حين قـابلنا أشخـاصاً في قلوبهم إيمان ذكروا لنا انهم كانوا يصومون سراً منذ سنوات ولكنهم لا يصلون، قالوا انهم لم يجدوا أحـداً يمكن ان يعلمـهم كـيف يؤدون الصلاة.

● كـانت الحكومـة الالبـانيـة السابقة تقمع أي شخص يحاول ان يمارس شـعـائره الدينـية.. هل الحكومة الحالية متسامحة مع المسلمين بشـأن أداء عـبـاداتهم واقامة المساجد؟

ـ نعم، فالحكومة الحالية في ألبانيا قد ازالت جميع العقبات التي كانت قد وضعتها الحكومة الشيوعية السابقة ومن ذلك منح المواطنين حرية العبادة واقامة المساجد الجديدة واصلاح المساجد القديمة والتعويض عن المساجد التي هدمت أو أزيلت، بل انها عـوضت المسلمين عن كثير من المساجد التي أزيلت بأراض حكومـيـة تقام عليهـا مساجد جديدة بديلة عن المساجد المهدومة، وفي بعض الحالات لم يستطع المسلمون إيجاد مصلى لهم، فأعطتهم الحكومـة الحالية مكاناً من البيـوت الحكومية مؤقتاً يقيمون فيه الصلاة، كما حدث في مدينة (دورس) التي كان فيها قبل الشيوعيين سبعة مساجد ازالها الشيوعيـون كلها بالجرافات والغوا أثرها، وعندما جاءت الحكومة الحاضرة لم يكن باستطاعة المسلمين بناء مكان يصلون فيه فاعطتهم الحكومة بيتا حكوميا مؤقتا، وحتى في بعض المدن أعطتهم مقرات فرع من فروع الحزب الشيوعي أو هيئاته لكي يتخذوه مسجدا مؤقتا.

● في السـابق كـان يوجد في البـانيـا تدريس الكتاتيب لتعليـم القـرآن الكريم.. هل عـادت هذه الكتاتيب مرة أخرى بعد انهيـار الشيـوعيـة.. وهل تجد من يقوم بالاشراف عليها؟

ـ لم يبدأ فتح الكتاتيب بعد، فـهي تحتاج الى مدرسين ولا يوجد مدرسون الآن يحسنون ان يدرسوا الأطفال وانما توجد فصول أو حلقات دراسية صغيرة في بعض المساجد لتعليم الاطفال تعليماً مـبـدئياً قليلاً لا تتـوافر له الوسـائل الناجحة التي من أهمها وجود المدرس والكتاب، ونرجو ان يتيسر ذلك قريبا.

al-Sharq al-Awsaṭ, 26 September 1991

CLASSROOM PRACTICE

5.1.5 *Written Exercise*

Skim through the two passages above silently.

1. What is the subject matter of the first passage?
2. What are the main topics discussed in the second passage?

● Editorials and comment columns

The syntax and vocabulary of editorials and comment columns are more varied than those of news items. The style of editorials, as in English newspapers, aspires to literariness:

جريدة العرب الدولية

قمة مجلس التعاون:

مسيرة يجب تسريعها

بعيداً عن اللقاءات الدبلوماسية لا بد من القول ان قمة مجلس التعاون الخليجي تجد السير نحو المفهوم العصري المتعارف عليه للتكامل الاقليمي.

هذا الكلام يحمل معنيين، وربما يفسر بانه سيف ذو حدين. ولا باس في هذا... لآن السير نحو تحقيق هذا النوع من التكامل سار بسرعة طيبة لكنها ليست السرعة التي تتحقق في تكامل مناطق عديدة من العالم لا تجمعها اهداف جامعة وقواسم مشتركة كتلك التي تجمع الدول الخليجية. ولعل مثل التقدم الذي يسجل على صعيد تكامل دول المجموعة الاوروبية مثل بديهي لما يمكن للمصلحة المشتركة ان تؤدي اليه، حتى بين دول ثرية كبرى تنازعت طويلا على اقتسام مناطق النفوذ على امتداد العالم وخاضت حربين عالميتين دمرتا اوروبا واسفرتا عن نظامين عالميين... ها نحن نشهد اليوم ثالثهما.

قد يقول قائل: ان في مقارنة تجربة الدول الخليجية الفتية بالدول الاوروبية اجحافاً لا يتوافق والموضوعية او الجدية التي يستحق ان تدرس بها هذه الحالة. وهذا صحيح.

بيد ان من الصحيح ايضاً ان منطقة الخليج بعد حربين ضاريتين، الاولى حصدت مئات الالوف من ابناء العراق وايران ودمرت اقتصادي البلدين واثبتت افلاس نظرية توسعية لا يقرها العالم ولا يطمئن اليها الانسان الخليجي والعربي، وثانيتهما كشفت هوية نظام عربي مغامر لم يكتف بابقاء وطنه الجريح في النفق المظلم بل حاول ادخال شعوب المنطقة كلها في هذا النفق، مما استدعى قيام جبهة عربية ودولية عريضة لتعيد الحق الى نصابه بموجب المبادئ الاخلاقية والانسانية ومواثيق الامم المتحدة التي لا تقر العدوان وترفض السماح للمعتدي بقطف ثمار عدوانه.

هاتان التجربتان برأينا اكثر من كافيتين لإنضاج الفهم السياسي والوعي المصلحي في المنطقة، خاصة انه تبلور تحديداً، في دمشق مع حرب نحرير الكويت، مفهوم مشترك جمع ما بين دول مجلس التعاون وتجاوزها الى دول اخرى لها تجربة غنية ومؤلمة في التصدي للعدوان والتوسع والقهر وقد احسن صائغو البيان الختامي لقمة مجلس التعاون في اعتباره اساس النظام العربي الجديد. هذا النظام لن ينتظر التردد ولن يعيش اذا ما بقيت رواسب الفردية ولا بد من تغذيته بالعمل المنظم الذي يستشرف الآفاق ويتعظ من التجارب والعبر.

«الشرق الاوسط»

al-Sharq al-Awasaṭ, 27 December 1991

Comment columns affect a chattier style:

ليس العرب وحدهم في الاعتقاد ان ثمة مؤامرة ضدهم، ففكرة المؤامرة هذه الايام في شيوع الفقر، ويندر ان يوجد بلد لا يعتقد شعبه ان ثمة مؤامرة، او مؤامرات ضده، بل انني اقرأ احياناً عن وجود مؤامرة يهودية دولية من النوع الذي آمن العرب بوجوده بعد سقوط النازية.

في بولندا ثمة اعتقاد شائع بأن اليهود يحاولون السيطرة على البلاد بعد سقوط الشيوعية. وطلب من المرشحين للانتخابات في اول تجربة ديموقراطية بعد الشيوعية ان يقسموا انهم وزوجاتهم لا يمارسون الطقوس اليهودية.

وهناك نظرية مؤامرة في بعض افريقيا السوداء خلاصتها ان الايدز انتشر عن طريق مؤامرة بين تل ابيب وبريتوريا ضد السود.

وكنت في واشنطن عندما انتشر فيها فجأة خبر مؤامرة لتفريغ العاصمة من سكانها السود، الذين يشكلون ٨٠ في المئة من السكان، مع حلول القرن القادم.

ويقول العلماء ان انتشار نظريات المؤامرة هذه الايام سببه سقوط الشيوعية، وبالتالي نظرية المؤامرة الشيوعية التي طغت على كل مؤامرة اخرى في حينها.

وتحمل كثرة المؤامرات المزعومة جانباً ايجابياً وآخر سلبياً بالنسبة الى العرب. فعلى الصعيد الايجابي لم يعد احد يستطيع ان يتهم العرب بأنهم وحدهم تالفو الاعصاب، او حتى مجانين. غير ان الجانب السلبي اخطر، فكثرة المؤامرات والنظريات عنها قد تعني انه لا توجد مؤامرة. والمثل الانكليزي يقول «اذا كان كل

انسـان مـهما فلا انسـان مهماً». والمعنى انه لا يعود ممكناً التفريق بين انسان وآخر عندما يستويان في الاهمية. وهكذا فقد يأتي يوم يصرخ فيه العرب «مؤامرة» فلا يصدقهم أحد لأن المؤامرات في كل مكان.

والاميركيون قد يجدون انفسهم في وضع اسوأ كثيرا من وضع العرب مع حرية الكلام الاسطورية التي يمارسونها، والتي تجـعل كل شيء مسموحاً.

الاميركيون اليوم يقولون ان ثمة مؤامرة يابانية للسيطرة على بلادهم، ويقولون ان ثمة مؤامرة باباوية للسيطرة على مؤسسات البـلاد وفرض الكثلكة عليها، ويقولون ان التـحـالف الصناعي – العسكري يبحث عن حرب مدمرة يجر البلاد اليها.

ولم يفد الوضع ان يوزع أخيراً فيـلم «جي إف كي» الذي آصر على وجود مؤامرة وراء اغتيال الرئيس جون كنيدي فأذكى نار كل مؤامرة أخرى.

وسط هذا الفيـض الاميـركي من نظريات المؤامرات أتوقف عند واحدة قد تضيع وسط الزحام هي نظرية وجود مؤامرة لاغـتيال جورج بوش.

وكان فيكتور اوستروفسكي عميل الموساد السابق ومؤلف كتاب «بطريق الخداع» بلّغ عضو الكونغرس السابق بول ماكلوسكي ان الموساد ربما تعد لاغتيال بوش المؤيد للعرب حتى يخلفه نائبه دان كويل المعروف بتأييده الكبير لاسرائيل، وان أنصار اسرائيل بدأوا عملية «تلميع» شخصية كويل فى جميع وسائط الاعلام تمهيداً لتـسـليمـه الحكم. وبلّغ مـاكلوسكي المخـابرات السـرية ووزارة الخارجية فضحكت عليه.

غير ان بول فندلي وهو عضو سابق آخر في الكونغرس، يحمل الرواية محمل الجد، ويقول ان من واجبات المخابرات التزام جانب الحذر المطلق.

كل مـا نرجوه ألا نرى فيلماً في السنوات القادمة عن بوش بعد كنيدي.

جهاد الخازن

● Specialist articles

A mixture of the above styles and formats will be found on the specialist pages. In addition, the arts/culture pages carry reviews and features couched in literary or academic language, as well as, frequently, poems, short stories and serialised extracts from historical or critical studies. Linguistically, such material falls outside the purview of this book, as does the Quranic, devotional and legal

material to be found on the religious pages. Sport receives wide
coverage in both the local and the international press, but, in most
international newspapers, the business section is by far the longest of
the special sections. The article opposite is a representative item.

HOMEWORK

1. Translate the second passage above (interview with an Albanian
   Muslim leader) into idiomatic English.
2. What is the topic of the editorial passage above from *al-Sharq al-
   Awsaṭ*, 27 December 1991?
3. (a) Find in the comment column from *al-Ḥayāh*, 31 January 1992,
   the Arabic terms corresponding to the English words/phrases given
   below, and use each in a complete Arabic sentence of your own:

   conspiracy – the idea of conspiracy – conspiracy theory

   (b) Summarise the passage in English.
4. Briefly analyse the style and presentation of the passage opposite
   from the business pages of *al-Ḥayāh*, 31 January 1992.
5. Use each of the following words/phrases in a complete Arabic
   sentence of your own:

قَمَعَ - عَن + ه + عَوَّضَ - اِسْتِثْناءٌ - سَيِّءٌ - مَصاعِبُ -
مُؤَقَّتاً - عَلَناً - سِرّاً - حرية العِبادة

al-Ḥayāh, 31 January 1992

أول مؤتمر اقتصادي في القاهرة لدعم قانون قطاع الأعمال

لازالة الغموض وايضاح بنود تطبيقه

القاهرة - عادل عبد العظيم:

■ عقد في القاهرة (يناير) بين ١٨ و٢٠ أول مؤتمر اقتصادي للاوراق المالية وبحث مؤتمر المصرية للاوراق المالية وتناقش مؤتمرو المصرية للاوراق المالية عقب الاعمال حضر الؤتمر مديرو عام الاحمال وتطبيقات وتنظيم قانون قطاع الاعمال، حضر المؤتمر ...

أحمد فؤاد أبو هيب، نجيب أن يوضح في الإعداد أن القانون الى هيئات القطاع العام واعاد تنظيم كل منها على شركات قابضة لتحقيق أهداف وأن القانون يسعى الى تحقيق شركات القطاع...

وقال الدكتور الاقتصادي السيد وموضحاته في هذا القانون وتحديث هيئة القانون وبحث خطيئته...

APPENDIX

Calendars

Dates quoted in newspapers and broadcasts are often given in two forms. For example:

‑ سينعقد المؤتمر العالمي للبيئة في حَزِيران (يونيو) ١٩٩٦ .

‑ تبدأ المناقشات في ٢١ ديسمبر (كانون الأول) الحالي .

That is, the western date is followed by the same date in the eastern solar/Christian calendar, or vice versa. (The combination of Muslim date/Christian date also occurs.) The eastern solar calendar is given below.

		Eastern
January	يناير	كانونُ الثاني
February	فبراير	شُباط
March	مارس	أذار
April	أبريل	نَيْسان
May	مايو	أيّار
June	يونيو	حَزِيران
July	يوليو	تَمّوز
August	أغسطس	أب
September	سبتمبر	أيْلول
October	أكتوبر	تِشْرِينُ الأول
November	نوفمبر	تِشْرِينُ الثاني
December	ديسمبر	كانونُ الأول

Variants on the above Arabic forms (both columns) are also found.
Libya has its own 'revolutionary' solar calendar.
Some North African newspapers use the western numerals 1, 2, 3 etc. in dates and elsewhere in preference to Arabic numerals.

Part II

Part II

Politics

This unit contains a small selection from the vocabulary of political life as reflected in the media. This skeleton vocabulary is used in drills designed to develop the following skills:

Lesson 6.1: acquiring vocabulary through listening;

Lesson 6.2: use of new vocabulary outside the framework of set translations;

Lesson 6.3: sustained oral translation out of Arabic; free oral translation into Arabic;

Lesson 6.4: (revision); sustained aural comprehension.

LESSON 6.1: POLITICAL CHANGE

The exercises in the Classroom Practice deal in broad terms with some of
the processes of leaving and coming to power; the Homework exercises
deal with changes of political outlook and regime.

CLASSROOM PRACTICE

6.1.1 *Aural/Oral Exercise*

Listen to the following passages, which will each be read aloud twice by
the teacher. In Arabic, orally, paraphrase or explain the words/phrases
stressed (underlined in the text) after the second reading.

۱ـ دعا السيد علي سالم البيض نائب رئيس مجلس الرئاسة
اليمني امس الى جعل ۱۹۹۲ "سنة <u>الانتقال الى</u> الديمقراطية" .

۲ـ انتهى الاجتماع بين رئيس الوزراء الباكستاني وزعماء
المجاهدين الافغان على إرسال وفد من المجاهدين الى مسكو لإجراء
محادثات <u>في شأن</u> مقترحات روسية رامية الى تشكيل <u>حكومة
انتقالية</u> .

۳ـ تم الاتفاق على إرسال وفد من المجاهدين الى مسكو لإجراء
محادثات في شأن مقترحات روسية رامية الى تشكيل <u>حكومة
مؤقّتة</u> .

٤ـ تم الاتفاق على إرسال وفد من المجاهدين الى مسكو لإجراء
محادثات في شأن مقترحات روسية رامية الى تشكيل <u>حكومة
ائْتلاف</u> انتقالية في كابل بمشاركة <u>عناصر</u> من الحكومة الحالية .

٥ـ قال الملك فهد في حديث لصحيفة "عكاظ" السعودية ان الموقف
الاسرائيلي لن <u>يحوّل</u> دون بذل المزيد من الجهد . وأعرب الملك فهد
عن أمله في ان تؤدي مفاوضات مدريد الى استمرار <u>الحوار</u> بين
<u>الأطراف المَعْنيّة</u> .

٦ـ طالب زعماء الاحزاب المعارضة التي <u>عُلّقت</u> السنة الماضية
بإعادة الديمقراطية .

6.1.2 Written/Oral Exercise

Listen to the following three passages, which will each be read aloud three times by the teacher:

(a) In Arabic, write down the words/phrases stressed (underlined in the text).

(b) Read the passages aloud and, in Arabic, paraphrase or explain the following words/phrases orally:

سياسيون ـ شكّل حزباً ـ اعتزل العملَ السياسيُّ ـ اعتزل الحياةَ
السياسيةَ ـ عزل + ه + من ـ الكنيست ـ عُضْوية ـ منافس ـ
أقام في

١ـ قال سياسيون من عدن انهم سيشكلون حزبا جديدا رغم إعلان
زعيمهم اعتزاله العمل السياسي . وأصدر السياسيون ، الذين
يقيمون في صنعاء ، بيانا قالوا فيه انهم سيشكلون حزبا
ديمقراطيا موحدا .

٢ـ قرر وزير الدفاع الإسرائيلي الأسبق عيزرا وايزمن اعتزال
الحياة السياسية والاستقالة من عضوية الكنيست الإسرائيلي.
جاء ذلك في تقرير ورد أمس من الأراضي العربية المحتلة .

٣ـ عزل رئيس الصومال المؤقت علي مهدي محمد منافسه
الجنرال فرح عيديد من رئاسة حزب المؤتمر الصومالي الموحد .

(c) Translate sentences 1–10 below orally into Arabic:

1. Mrs Thatcher has announced that she is leaving politics.
2. Thatcher retires at last!
3. A number of British politicians have welcomed Mrs Thatcher's announcement that she is to leave politics at the end of the year.
4. Several politicians have recently announced that they are leaving the Socialist Party.
5. The head of the provisional government has fired his minister of the interior.
6. He said that rivalry between the minister of the interior and army leaders had led to the threat of war.
7. The provisional government's main rival in the power struggle now taking place in the country is the Free United Democratic Socialist Party, whose leader lives in Paris.

8. The former Defence Minister says he will resign from the Israeli parliament and leave politics before the elections.
9. The house is being used temporarily as the headquarters of the provisional government.
10. At a press conference, the minister, who was sacked yesterday, said he was leaving politics to spend more time with his family, and that the government would continue to received his backing.

6.1.3 Aural/Written Exercise

Listen to the following passages, which will each be read aloud three times by the teacher.

1. In Arabic, write down the words/phrases stressed (underlined in the text) and any other terms that are new to you.
2. Write an English summary of each passage after the third reading.

١_ رحبت مصادر دبلوماسية في اليونان امس باحتمال تأجيل موعد الاجتماع الايطالي البلغاري المقرر عقده في اثينا اواخر الشهر الحالي الى وقت آخر خلال الشهر المقبل . وقالت المصادر ان سبب تأجيل الاجتماع يعود الى التطورات السياسية في كل من ايطاليا وبلغاريا و وصول رئيسين جديدين للسُّلْطة في كل منهما فضلا عن تطورات سياسية محتملة في بلغاريا .

٢_ اتهم زعيم الحزب الاتحادي الديمقراطي السوداني في رسالة وجهها الى رئيس نيجيريا الجبهة الاسلامية بأنها استولت على السُّلْطة لمنع حل قضية الحرب في الجنوب .

6.1.4 Oral Exercise

Translate the following passage into Arabic, section by section:

The general came to power last month after a long power struggle between military and civilian leaders. / He seized power after sacking his civilian rival, the caretaker prime minster, / and upon seizing power declared that the main problem facing the country was that of resolving the current economic crisis. / He called for a coalition between all parties concerned, including civilian politicians and parties and the military, / and proposed the formation of a transitional government comprising elements from the previous regime. /

However, the political parties have refused to cooperate or engage in a dialogue with the military regime. / As a result, the general has threatened to suspend all political parties. / He insists publicly that he supports democracy, / and has held a series of talks with other leaders in the region with the aim of asserting the legitimacy of his regime, / but it is believed in the capital that he is secretly holding negotiations with foreign military experts, / and is said to have bought a large number of helicopters and other military aircraft. / However, he does not have the entire support of the army, / and has already crushed a number of plots in which leading military figures are believed to have taken part. /

Meanwhile, the country is in an even worse state than before, / and the international community has called for increased efforts to end the state of undeclared war in the north. / But as the country's former leader, who now lives in Paris, has pointed out, / international pressure is unlikely to change the general's position. / Indeed, the former leader has accused several western countries of secretly supporting the new regime, / adding that the difficulties which his country currently faces are largely due to western support for the previous regime. / – In the last few minutes, news has reached us that the general has dissolved all political parties, suspended parliament, and openly declared war on all elements who oppose his rule.

HOMEWORK

1. Compile a list of the Arabic terms relating to politics that have been used in Units 1–5.
2. Read the following passages, but do not translate them.

ـ اعلن سياسيون في جنوب السودان عن اقتراحهم **فصل الجنوب عن** الشمال . وبينما رفضت الحكومة السودانية التعليق على المقترحات قال الرئيس السوداني السابق جعفر نميري ان الدول الافريقية لن تقبل فصل الجنوب السوداني واشار الى ان اعلان دولة **انفصالية** في شمال السودان لم يجد مؤيدا حتى اليوم على الرغم من ان ذلك اعلن في ايار (مايو) ١٩٩٠ .

ـ اكد الملك الحسن الثاني ان قضايا **احترام حقوق الانسان** في البلاد ستعرف قريبا **طَفْرة نَوْعية** "تحول المغرب الى **مَضْرِب مَثَلٍ** في هذا الشأن".

(a) Use each of the five words/phrases underlined in a complete Arabic sentence of your own.
(b) Translate your Arabic sentences into idiomatic English.

3. Read the following passages, but do not translate them.

ـ عزل رئيس الصومال المؤقت علي مهدي محمد منافسه الجنرال محمد فرح عيديد من رئاسة حزب المؤتمر الصومالي الموحد. وكان عيديد قد نُصب رئيسا للمؤتمر الصومالي الموحد بعد محادثات السلام التي جرت في جيبوتي في يوليو (تموز) الماضي من اجل انهاء المنافسات الفئوية، لكنه انشق بعد ذلك بأربعة اشهر ليطالب برئاسة الدولة .

ـ وصف قادة "التجمع الوطني الديمقراطي" السوداني مؤتمرهم الذي انعقد في لندن بأنه "تاريخي ونقطة تحوّل في المقاومة ضد النظام". واشاروا الى انهم اقروا برنامج عمل لمواصلة "المقاومة الشعبية لإسقاط نظام الجبهة الاسلامية العسكري الذي استولى على السلطة في انقلاب ٣٠ يونيو (حزيران) ١٩٨٩ واعادة الديمقراطية" .

وقد دعا "التجمع الوطني الديمقراطي" المعارض في نهاية مؤتمره امس مجلس الثورة السوداني الى "حل نفسه وتسليم السلطة. واستبعد التجمع اي حديث عن الانفصال واتفق على وحدة السودان والحكم اللا مركزي .

Use the vocabulary which they contain to write one or more Arabic news stories of your own around the following words/phrases:

faction/factional – to split off – decentralised rule – revolution – coup – turning point – to resist/resistance – to hand over power – to dissolve itself – to topple a regime

---

REVISION

1. Translate 6.1.4 Oral Exercise orally at speed.
2. In Arabic, orally, take it in turns to explain briefly the following terms and use each in a complete Arabic sentence which illustrates its meaning:

فئة / فئوي ـ انشق ـ الحكم اللا مركزي ـ نقطة تحول ـ ثورة ـ انقلاب ـ مقاومة ـ سلّم السلطة ـ حلّ نفسه ـ أسقط نظاما

LESSON 6.2: PARTIES AND ELECTIONS

The exercises in the Classroom Practice deal with western parties and elections; the Homework exercises deal with elections in non-western countries and other forms of government response to pressure from the electorate.

CLASSROOM PRACTICE

6.2.1 Aural/Oral Exercise

Listen to the following passage, which will be read aloud twice by the teacher. At the second reading, the teacher will paraphrase or explain the words and phrases stressed (underlined in the text) in Arabic.

1. Write down the Arabic terms and their English equivalents.
2. Listen to the passage being read aloud a third time, section by section, by the teacher. Translate each section orally into English.

ديمقراطية الـغـرب فـي أزمة: / بـعـض المعلومات عـن الانتخابات فـي
اميركا وفـي بـريطانيا /

يشير استطلاع رأي أجري حديثا في الولايات المتحدة الى ان هناك
عددا كبيرا مـن النـاخبين الاميركيين الذين لا يشاركون فـي
الانتخابات / وقد بـلـغ نسبتهم حَوالَى ثلثي الناخبين / وهي الى
ازدياد. / وتجري الحملات الانتخابية / ويتم الاقتراع / من دون
اي نقاش جادّ للقضايا الرئيسية / مهما كان تأثير هذه القضايا
على حياة النـاخبين. / ويتم ترشيح المرشّحين وانتخابهم على
اساس الصورة التي تتكون حولهم في وسائل الاعلام. / وتتضاءل
مـع الوقت الفوارق بـين الحزبين المتصارعين وهما الحزب
الديمقراطي والحزب الجمهوري / كما تتضاءل فـي بريطانيا
الفوارق بـين حزب العُمّال وحزب المحافظين. / ويضم كل من حزب
المحافظين وحزب العمال في بريطانيا والحزب الجمهوري والحزب
الديمقراطي فـي اميركا الليبيراليين والمحافظين مـعا / مما يخفف
مـن الفوارق بـين الحزبين الرئيسيين في كل من الولايات المتحدة
وبـريطانيا / حتى يكاد ان يتم الانتخاب على اساس بُروز شخصية

المرشح / وليس على اساس الحزب الذي ينتمي اليه. / ومع ذلك
فنادرا ما يفوز المرشحون المستقلون في الانتخابات. / وبما ان
الانتخاب يتم على اساس الاشخاص اكثر مما يتم على اساس
الاحزاب والقضايا / يصبح من الواضح ان الاحزاب لم تعد تعني
كثيرا . / ويقول بعض علماء السياسة ان الحزب الاكثر اتساعا
ونموا في كل من بريطانيا والولايات المتحدة هو "حزب غير
الناخبين" .

al-Ḥayāh, 14 November 1990

6.2.2 Oral Exercise

Translate the following sentences into Arabic:

1. The two main parties in Britain are the Labour Party and the Conservative Party.
2. An opinion poll conducted recently indicates that the fastest-growing party in Scotland is the Scottish Nationalist Party.
3. Do you belong to a party, and do you vote? I'm a non-voter myself.
4. Around half the British electorate don't vote in general elections. The British electorate is a byword in this respect.
5. Local elections are generally held in March.
6. Election campaigns are still much more important in the USA than in Britain.
7. Parties and party membership no longer mean much in the States.
8. The important thing is the candidate's media image.
9. The contending parties rarely debate issues and policies, and some voters say there is no longer any real difference between them.
10. Nevertheless, independent candidates rarely get elected; you need party support to win an election.

6.2.3 Oral/Written Exercise

In Arabic, using complete sentences, define the following terms, first orally and then in writing:

democracy – elections – parliament – opinion poll – debate

6.2.4 Oral Exercise

In Arabic, explain the following terms, either singly or, where appropriate, in contrasting or complementary pairs:

Labour – Conservative – Ulster Unionist – Scottish Nationalist –
Monster Raving Loony Party

general election/by-election – local election/parliamentary election –
president/prime minister (in a republic) – constitutional monarch/prime
minister (in a constitutional monarchy) – issue/policy – personality/
media image – party candidate/independent candidate

6.2.5 *Written Exercise*

In Arabic, using complete sentences, briefly define or explain the above
pairs.

HOMEWORK

1. Write one or more complete Arabic sentences of your own using the
   following words/phrases in any order you wish:

نسبة ـ نقاش جاد ـ إلى ازدياد ـ تضاءل ـ خفّف من ـ
مَهْما ـ مِمّا ـ بما أنّ ـ نموّ ـ اتسع

2. Read the following passages, but do not translate them.

ـ إعلان حال للطوارئ لـ ١٢ شهرا في الجزائر
والجيش يعلق المقر الرئيسي لجبهة الإنقاذ

أبلغ المجلس الأعلى للدولة في الجزائر امس زعماء الأحزاب في
البلاد انه اتخذ إجراءات استثنائية لوضع حد لأعمال العنف .
وأبرز هذه الإجراءات إعلان حال الطوارئ "لمدة ١٢ شهرا ويمكن
رفعها قبل هذا الموعد" إذا تحسنت الاوضاع .

ـ تعديل وزاري وشيك في الأردن

علم في عمان ان تعديلا وزاريا سيطرا على وزارة السيد زين بن
شاكر خلال الايام القليلة المقبلة . واكد مصدر مطلع ان التعديل
سيشمل خروج السيد باسل جردانة وزير المالية من الوزارة ،
بينما سيتولى الدكتور عبد الله النسور وزير الصناعة والتجارة
الحالي حقيبة وزارة المالية بدلا من وزارة الصناعة والتجارة .

(a) Use each of the six words/phrases underlined in a complete
Arabic sentence of your own.
(b) Translate your Arabic sentences into idiomatic English.

(c) Write an Arabic news story of your own using the following words/phrases in any order you wish:

وضع حدّاً لأعمال العنف ـ تحسّن ـ وشيك ـ طرأ على ـ بدلاً من

3. Read the following passages, but do not translate them.

ـ ذكر احد ثوّار بورما ان المعارضة البورمية ، التي أحرزت انتصارا ساحقا في انتخابات مايو الماضي، قد تعلن حكومة مؤقتة في المناطق التي يسيطر عليها الثوّار .

ـ بوتو تجدد اتهاماتها بتزوير الانتخابات

انتخبت الجمعية الوطنية في باكستان نواز شريف ، زعيم التحالف الديمقراطي ، رئيسا جديدا للحكومة الباكستانية . وحصل شريف على ١٥٣ صوتا في الجمعية التي تضم ٢١٧ مقعدا. وتشكل الغالبية الساحقة التي حصل عليها شريف ما يزيد على ثلثي الاصوات اللازمة في الجمعية الوطنية لإجراء تغييرات دستورية . واتهمت رئيسة الوزراء السابقة بي نظير بوتو الحكومة الانتقالية، التي نُصبت عقب قيام الرئيس غلام اسحاق خان بإقالتها ، بتزوير الانتخابات .

Use the vocabulary that they contain to write one or more Arabic news stories of your own around the following words/phrases:

to dismiss – to rig the elections – to appoint – to win (a certain number of) votes – to win a crushing victory – to secure an overwhelming majority – seat (in parliament) – to control – insurgent – alliance

---

REVISION

6.2.6 Oral Exercise

In Arabic, orally, take it in turns to explain briefly the following terms and use each in a complete Arabic sentence which illustrates its meaning:

حال الطوارئ ـ تعديل وزاري ـ تزوير الانتخابات ـ إجراءات استثنائية ـ تولى حقيبةً ـ سيطر على ـ ثائر ـ تحالفُ ـ أقال ـ مقعد

6.2.7 Oral Exercise

Translate the following passage into Arabic, section by section:

Since the military coup last year, a number of factions have emerged or re-emerged in the country. / Communist insurgents control several areas; / they are demanding decentralised rule / and have called on the government to hand over power to the local Committees of the People's Revolution. / They say that if elections are held, the government will only rig them. / The government for its part says that there is no need for it to hold elections / because it would win a crushing victory and secure an overwhelming majority. / The United Democratic People's Party has called for elections to be held as soon as possible, / declaring that if it came to power, democracy would experience a quantum leap / which would transform the country into a byword for human rights. / The main issue facing the military regime is that of separatism. / Several factions representing different regions have set up provisional separatist governments, / and have called on the people throughout the country to resist the government. / Meanwhile, several factions within the ruling party itself have split off from it / and have called on the people to topple the regime; / they are believed to be behind the recent acts of violence in the capital. / The government has adopted a number of extraordinary measures / in an attempt to end the violence, / and it is reported that a cabinet reshuffle is imminent. / It is expected that the Minister of Tourism will take over the Ministry of Culture, / and some observers say that the government is about to invite elements of the old regime / to take part in an alliance with it and form a coalition government.

LESSON 6.3: POLITICAL TRENDS; POLITICAL APPOINTMENTS

The exercises in the Classroom Practice deal with electoral issues from the standpoint of parties and of the public; the Homework exercises deal with broad political trends and with appointments to government and to the legislature.

CLASSROOM PRACTICE

6.3.1 *Aural/Oral Exercise*

Listen to the following passage, which will be read aloud once, the stressed items (underlined in the text) being repeated once or twice by the teacher.

1. Listen to the same passage being read aloud a second time, section by section. As you listen, translate each section orally into English. Guess the meaning of any unfamiliar terms.
2. Listen to the passage being read aloud section by section a third time. In Arabic, give an explanatory paraphrase of each section.

تتواصل المشاورات بين عدد من الشخصيات الموريتانية المستقلة / التي لم تعلن حتى الآن انتماءها لحزب سياسي / والتي تعرف بـــ ولائها لـ لمرشح السابق لرئاسة الجمهورية أحمد ولد داداه ./ وقد أعلنت انها توشك على تشكيل حزب سياسي مقرب من ولد داداه / يستطيع جمع كل الذين أيدوه في الانتخابات الرئاسية الأخيرة / خارج مظلّة الأحزاب ./ ويلعب سيدي ولد أحمد دي مدير الحملة الانتخابية لولد داداه دورا كبيرا في تشكيل الحزب الجديد ./

و يخشى المراقبون من ان يؤثر الحزب الجديد على استمرار وجود حزب الاتحاد القومي الديمقراطي/المعروف حتى الآن بأنه التكتل الرئيسي لقوى المعارضة الموريتانية ./ إلا ان الناطق الرسمي باسم حزب الاتحاد القومي الديمقراطي/ يرى انه لا وجود لمنافسة بين تنظيمه و الحزب المراد تشكيله / فكل واحد له برنامجه .

ودعا زعيم حزب الاتحاد القومي الديمقراطي الى إجراء انتخابات حرة ونظيفة قبل نهاية السنة / وأشار الى انه "من غير الممكن

سياسيا / تأجيل هذه <u>العملية</u> / و <u>حرمان</u> الشعب الموريتاني <u>من</u> ان يكون له لأول مرة في تاريخه / مجلس يمثّله في إطار التعددية." /. وأشار قادة الحزب المراد تشكيله الى تحقيق <u>تقدم</u> في عدة جوانب مهمة / منها <u>الإجماع على</u> دولة ديمقراطية تعددية / "تعكس التعددية الثقافية لأهل موريتانيا".

6.3.2 *Oral Exercise*

Listen to the following passage, which will be read aloud once by the teacher. Next, listen to the passage being read aloud again, section by section, and translate it orally into Arabic.

Adopt whatever (non-colloquial) style you wish, paraphrase unfamiliar terms, and abridge or pad where necessary to achieve a fluent transation. Repeat the exercise, if necessary, until fluency is achieved.

X: Professor Jasper Nossiter is a well-known expert on contemporary British politics and psephology / whom we have invited here today to give us his views on the run-up to the forthcoming general election. / Professor Nossiter, what differences are there, if any, between the packages which the two main parties are offering the electorate? /

N: Many observers are saying that neither party has come up with a coherent, identifiable package. / In the absence of identifiable policies, the election is bound to be a matter of personalities. /

X: Is this going to be an American-style election campaign? / What are candidates doing to try and project their personalities? /

N: Well, the best example is Screaming Lord Sutch and the Monster Raving Loony Party. /

X: Rather a unique example. Are you suggesting that other politicians should adopt a similar profile? /

N: Obviously not. Independent candidates are responsible for their own image. / Party candidates have to adopt a personal image which conforms to the party image. / This is more difficult for opposition candidates, who also have to try and be all things to all men. /

X: What about the party manifestos? / A candidate can't promise devolution for Scotland if it's not in the party manifesto. /

N: The party manifesto isn't a hard-and-fast agenda. / Anyway, a candidate can always point out that there is a much better chance of devolution if his or her party is returned. /

X: There are some issues, like devolution, like women's issues, which cut across traditional party loyalties. / Do you think that women's issues, for example, are going to play a major role in this election? /

N: There is no doubt that this is a card which both main parties will try to play. / But although women form over half the electorate, frankly I can't see this becoming a major electoral issue.

HOMEWORK

1. Write one or more complete Arabic sentences of your own using the following words/phrases in any order you wish:

مظلّة الأحزاب ـ ولاء ـ انتخابات رئاسية ـ مدير حملة انتخابية ـ
تكتّل ـ حرم + ه + من (حرم + ه + هـ) / حِرمان ـ تقدّمُ ـ
أجمع على ـ انتخابات حرة ونظيفة

2. (a) Read the following passages, but do not translate them. Use the terms underlined in one or more complete Arabic sentences of your own.

ـ نُصِبت حكومة انتقالية عقب قيام الرئيس الباكستاني غلام اسحاق خان بإقالة بي نظير بوتو من مَنْصِب رئاسة الوزراء .

ـ أعلنت ماغرت ثاتشر أمس في اجتماع لمجلس الوزراء عزمها على الاستقالة من منصب رئاسة الوزراء .

ـ السيدة ليلى شرف هي المرأة الأولى والوحيدة التي عُيّنت في مجلس الأعْيان الأردني بعد الانتخابات الأخيرة . وأدلت بحديث للصحف بعد تعيينها قالت فيه : "كنت أتمنى ان تكون هناك أكثر من امرأة في مجلس الأعيان ليصبح دور المرأة ومشاركتها في الحياة السياسية العامة أمرا طبيعيا". وقالت "سيكون لي اهتمام خاص بالقضايا التي تتعلق بالمرأة".

ـ أفادت الأنباء الواردة من بيروت بأن سليم الحص رئيس وزراء لبنان أعلن عن استقالة حكومته . ومن المتوقع ان يتولى عمر كرامي رئاسة الحكومة . وسيعلن عن تعيين رسمي قريبا .

- قد **شغل** الدكتور أحمد محمد الاصبحي عدة **مناصب** وزارية،
من بينها وزير الصحة العامة في اليمن الشمالي سابقا قبل ان
يصبح أمينا عاما للمؤتمر الشعبي إضافةً الى عضويته في
المجلس المستشاري .

(b) Read the following passages, but do not translate them. Find the
different terms used to designate elective and non-elective chambers.

- السيدة ليلى شرف هي المرأة الاولى والوحيدة التي عيّنت في
مجلس الأعْيان الاردني . وادلت بحديث للصحف بعد تعيينها قالت
فيه : "كنت أتمنى ان تكون هناك اكثر من امرأة في مجلس
الأعْيان".

- طالب الرئيس السابق لمجلس النوّاب الكويتي الذي علّق عام ١٩٨٦
بإعادة الديمقراطية .

- اعلن زعيم التيّار المتشدد في ايران والنائب في المجلس النيابي
علي أكبر محتشمي امس ان المشاركة في مؤتمر مدرير للسلام "هي
اعلان حرب على الاسلام" .

- عبّر رئيس الحكومة الجزائرية عن امله في ان يعطيه المجلس
الشعبي الوطني امكانيات اجراء انتخابات تشريعية حرة ونظيفة
قبل آخر السنة .

- ابلغ المجلس الأعْلى للدولة في الجزائر امس زعماء الاحزاب في
البلاد انه اتخذ اجراءات استثنائية لوضع حد لأعمال العنف .

- رئيس البرلمان المغربي يدعو الى انتخابات تشريعية حرة
ونزيهة في الجزائر

(c) In Arabic, explain briefly or give synonyms for the following words/phrases:

اجتماع لمجلس الوزراء ـ عزم على ـ تمنى ـ وحيد ـ نائب ـ انتخابات تشريعية ـ انتخابات حرة ونزيهة

3. Read the following passages, but do not translate them:

ـ قال الملك فهد في حديث لصحيفة "عكاظ" السعودية ان المواقف الاسرائيلية المتصلبة لن تحول دون بذل المزيد من الجهد .

ـ اعلن زعيم التيار المتشدد في ايران والنائب في المجلس النيابي علي أكبر محتشمي امس ان المشاركة في مؤتمر مدريد للسلام "هي اعلان حرب على المسلمين". وقال ان المشاركين فيه "محكوم عليهم بالإعدام وسيُعدمون" مضيفا ان ما وصفهم بـ "الثوريين" سيقومون بـ "واجبهم" إزاء "أعْداء الاسلام في اقرب وقت ومهما كانت الظروف" .

ـ حقق الاسلاميون فوزا بارزا في الانتخابات النقابية الاخيرة في الكويت ، إذ حصلوا على ٥٥ في المئة من اصوات المقترعين . وحصل الاسلاميون الشيعة على ١٧ في المئة من الاصوات . وحصل "الوسط الديمقراطي" الذي يمثل التيار العَلْماني على ١٣ في المئة من الاصوات ، وحصل "الاتحاد الاسلامي" الذي يمثل الاسلاميين السَلَفيّين على ١٠ في المئة من الاصوات .

ـ في استطلاع خاص بـ "الشرق الاوسط"
غزة: لا للتطرف ... نعم للسلام
كشف استطلاع رأي أجرته "الشرق الاوسط" في قطاع غزة ان ٦١ ٪ من السكان الفلسطينيين يؤيدون انعقاد مؤتمر السلام ويتمنون له النجاح .

ـ اقترح عدد من النواب في الكنيست الاسرائيلي اجراءات قد تؤدي الى حرمان عدد من الاحزاب الدينية المتطرفة واليمينية المتطرفة واليسارية المعارضة من اي تمثيل لها في الكنيست .

ـ استبعدت مصادر في جناحي "الحركة الشعبية لتحرير السودان"
امس ان تنعقد مفاوضات السلام بين الحكومة و "الحركة". ويذكران
الطرفين اعلنا منتصف الشهر الماضي رغبتهما في التفاوض لإنهاء
الحرب الدائرة في جنوب البلاد منذ سنوات لكن اعلان الانشقاق
في صفوف قيادة "الحركة" اجل عقد المفاوضات .

Use the vocabulary that they contain to write one or more Arabic news
stories of your own around the following words/phrases:

tendency – centre – hard-line – wing – right-wing – left-wing –
revolutionary – extremism/extremist – Islamic fundamentalist – secularist

---

REVISION

6.3.3 *Oral Exercise*

In Arabic, orally, take it in turns to explain briefly the following terms/
phrases and use each in a complete Arabic sentence which illustrates its
meaning:

قام بواجبه ـ محكوم عليه بالإعدام ـ إسلامي سَلَفيّ ـ ثَوْريّ ـ
متطرِّف ـ متشدِّد ـ متصلِّب ـ عَلْمانيّ ـ تيّار ـ وسط

LESSON 6.4: POLITICAL PROCEDURES

The exercises in the Classroom Practice are revision exercises which deal
in detail with specific electoral procedures; the Homework exercises
provide some additional vocabulary on elections and parliamentary procedure.

CLASSROOM PRACTICE

6.4.1 *Written/Oral Exercise*

1. Listen to the following passage, which will be read aloud twice,
   section by section, by the teacher. As you listen, write an English
   translation of the passage. Make a note of any unfamiliar terms and
   guess their meaning.

2. Check your translations against the text below, and discuss any
   points of difficulty.

3. Using your corrected translations, translate the passage back into
   Arabic orally, section by section.

بطرس غالي أول مرشح عن المجموعة العربية ينافس على منصب
الأمين العام للأمم المتحدة /

مع دخول عملية اختيار الأمين العام للأمم المتحدة مرحلتها
النهائية / بطرس غالي أول مرشح عن المجموعة العربية ينافس عن
المنصب /

دخلت عملية اختيار الأمين العام للأمم المتحدة مرحلتها الأخيرة /
ولأول مرة منذ نشأة المنظمة الدولية عام ١٩٤٥ / يتقدم عربي
للترشيح لهذا المنصب الكبير/ وهو الدكتور بطرس غالي نائب
رئيس الوزراء المصري لشؤون الاتصالات الخارجية./ فثمّة اتفاق
على ان الدكتور غالي ليس مجرد مرشح للقارّة الاقريقية / رغم
انها التي تقدمت بترشيحه عبر منظمة الوحدة الافريقية / وانما
هو ايضاً مرشح العرب ./ ومع ذلك فالواضح ان المنافسة على هذا
المنصب قوية للغاية ./

يتوقف اختيار الأمين العام على اتفاق الدول الخمس ذات العضوية الدائمة في مجلس الأمن عليه / اضافة الى حصوله على أربعة أصوات أخرى ـ على الأقل ـ/ من الدول العشر الأخرى غير دائمة العضوية في المجلس / وعندئذ يتقدم المجلس بتوصيته الى الجمعية العامة للتصويت عليها . / والمرشحون الأفارقة للمنصب أغلبية بين الذين أعلن ترشيحهم رسميا / حيث يوجد خمسة آخرون بخلاف الدكتور بطرس غالي/ الذي يعدّ أبرزهم وأكثرهم فرصة . / ولا تضم قائمة المرشحين غير اثنين آخرين من خارج افريقيا / هما وزير خارجية الفليبين ورئيسة وزراء النرويج .

al-Sharq al-Awasaṭ, 3 October 1991

6.4.2 Written/Oral Exercise

1. Listen to the following passage, which will be read aloud twice by the teacher. Write down the words/phrases stressed (underlined in the text) and, in Arabic, explain them briefly orally (use synonyms, antonyms, paraphrases or examples).
2. Listen to the passage being read aloud a third time, section by section. Orally, given an explanatory paraphrase of each section in Arabic.

أثار ترشيح الحزب الوطني الديمقراطي الحاكم في مصر سيدات أربع فقط من بين ٤٤٤ مرشحا في انتخابات مجلس الشعب المقبلة في مصر ردود فعل غاضبة في الأوساط السياسية و النسائية،/ إذ اعتبر البعض تلك الخطوة تراجعا عن الخطوات التي حققتها المرأة المصرية في المشاركة في القرار السياسي ./

التقت "الحياة" ثلاثة من العناصر النسائية البارزة في مصر وناقشتهن في قضية "مشاركة المرأة في العمل السياسي" ./ الدكتور سهير القلماوي ، عضو مجلس الشعب السابق، ترى ان "اشتراك المرأة في العمل السياسي لا بد ان يأتي من المرأة وليس مدفوعا من الدولة والاحزاب ،/وإن كانت الدولة في مراحل سابقة تشجّع تمثيل المرأة داخل مجلس الشعب"./

وتقول : لكنني لا أؤمن ـ بكل أسف ـ بوجود قضية للمرأة في مصر، بمعنى ان قضية المرأة هي قضية المجتمع ككلِ ./ فإنني

اعتقد ان العمل السياسي ككل يحتاج الى ثورة **جِذْرية** . / لأن المفهوم الآن لدى أغلب الناس ان العمل السياسي يمارَس فقط في الانتخابات وداخل مجلس الشعب ، / في حين ان **كل ما يتصل بالحياة هو من صميم العمل السياسي** . /

أما بالنسبة للدور السياسي للمرأة المصرية فاعتقد انها مازالت تمارس دورها في **الحياة العامة** و **الإدارات الحكومية** و **المؤسسات الاجتماعية** . / ووجود المرأة في المجتمع لا يجب ان **ينعكس على** عدد الأعضاء داخل مجلس الشعب **طالما انّ** هذا المجلس سيقوم بدوره في **معالجة مصالح المرأة** . /

وتقول الفنانة فايدة كامل المرشحة لمجلس الشعب المقبل للمرة السادسة **على التَّوالي** : انني أؤكد ان الأهمية ليست بعدد مقاعد المرأة داخل المجلس ، بل الأهم من ذلك هو **النَّشاط** الذي تقوم به المرأة داخل المجلس . /

أما الدكتورة فوزية عبد الستّار، استاذة القانون في جامعة القاهرة وعضو مجلس الشعب السابق، فترى ان الرجل قد **يصلح أكثر من المرأة في الدِّعاية** الانتخابية لنفسه / والتقرب من **أبناء دائرته.** / **فمهما قلنا عن تطور فكر الرجل العصري** إلا انه يجب ان نعترف انه لا يزال هناك بعض التقاليد الشرقية / التي تجعل كثيرا من الرجال **يترددون في تفضيل المرأة على الرجل.** /

وتؤكد الدكتورة فوزية عبد الستار: انه ليس من الممكن **إصدار قانون** يحدد عددا **معيَّنًا** من المقاعد للنساء ، كما حدث في الماضي ، / لأن هذا التحديد أصبح **غير دستوري** لأنه لا **يساوي بين** المرأة والرجل . / ولذلك فتحديد نسبة معيّنة للنساء **على غرار النسبة المخصصة للعمال والفلاحين** يحتاج الى تعديل دستوري . /

ومن أهم العوامل التي أدت الى ضآلة عدد النساء في مجلس الشعب عامل عدم إشراك المرأة في الأحزاب السياسية بأعداد كبيرة وبصورة ايجابية ./ ولذلك يجب التركيز على تعليم المرأة المصرية ، الأمر الذي يسمح بـ اتساع القاعدة الشعبية النيابية للمرأة ./ ومن ثُمَّ يزيد عدد النساء في مجلس الشعب .

al-Ḥayāh, 5 November 1990

HOMEWORK

1. Use the following words/phrases in one or more complete Arabic sentences of your own:

ثُمَّةَ ـ مجلس الأمن ـ الجمعية العامة ـ نشأة ـ مرحلة ـ توقف على ـ توصية ـ عُدَّ

2. Use the following words/phrases to write one or more brief Arabic news stories of your own:

من ثُمَّ ـ على غِرار ... ـ معيَّن ـ دعاية ـ شجّع + ه + على ـ عامل ـ جَذريّ ـ مَصْلَحة ـ ركّزَ على ـ على التَّوالي ـ قاعدة ـ ساوى بين ... و ... ـ ضآلة ـ دائرة ـ عَالَجَ

3. Translate 6.4.2 Aural/Oral Exercise into idiomatic English.
4. (a) Read the following passages, but do not translate them:

ـ يؤكد المراقبون في الجزائر عزم السلطات الجزائرية على عدم السماح للمعارضة الأصولية التونسية بالنَّشاط من داخل الجزائر ضد النظام التونسي .

ـ أشار قادة "التجمع الوطني الديمقراطي" الى تحقيق تقدم في عدة جوانب مهمة منها الاجماع على دولة ديمقراطية تعددية "تعكس التعددية الدينية والثقافية والعِرقية والقَبَلية لأهل السودان".

ـ فاز "الإخوان المسلمون" والمتعاطفون معهم بأكثر من ثلث مقاعد المجلس في الانتخابات الأخيرة .

Use the vocabulary that they contain to write an Arabic news story of your own around the following words/phrases:

to sympathise with/sympathiser – fundamentalist – racial – tribal – authorities

(b) Read the following passages, but do not translate them:

ـ اعلنت ماغرت ثاتشر امس في اجتماعٍ لمجلس الوزراء عزمها على الاستقالة من منصب رئاسة الوزراء فَوْرَ انتخابات زعيم جديد لحزب المحافظين . وكانت ثاتشير واجهت عُزْلة في اوروبا وشهدت تراجعا في شعبيتها في استطلاعات الرأي، خصوصا بسبب ترددها في اتخاذ الخطوات المؤدية الى الوحدة الاوروبية .

ـ يبدو ان تردد السلطات الجزائرية في اتخاذ الاجراءات لتقْيِيد حركة الأصوليين التونسيين سبّب التَّدَهْوُر الجديد في العلاقات الثنائية بين البلدين .

ـ حكومة ايرلندا تنجح في اقتراع ثقة على رغم التَّدَهْوُر في شعبيتها

ـ اتهم وزيرالدولة المغربي للشؤون الخارجية منظمات طُلّابية بــ "الإساءة الى صورة البلاد في الخارج".

Use the vocabulary that they contain to write an Arabic news story of your own around the following words/phrases:

popularity – breakdown/decline – to harm the image of – isolation – vote of confidence

5. Read the following passages, but do not translate them.

ـ ان الانتخابات الأردنية تمثل إرادة أقل من نصف الأردنيين . فعدد المسجَّلين في قوائم الاقتراع كان مليونا وتسعة عشر ألفا وثمانمائة واثنين وخمسين ناخبا وناخبة وعدد الذين اقترعوا لم يزد عن ٥١٠ آلاف ، اي ان نسبة الذين اقترعوا من المسجَّلين في القوائم تزيد قليلا عن ٥٠ في المئة .

ـ ان الكثير من السياسيين الجزائريين بما في ذلك عدد مهم من رجال النظام يبدون متشائمين في شأن إلغاء الانتخابات .

ـ دعا عدد مهم من النواب الى حل المجلس وإجراء انتخابات مبكّرة .

ـ سيؤجل بحث مشروع قانون تقدم به عدد من النواب المستقلين الى الدورة البرلمانية المقبلة .

ـ بحث النواب مشروع قانون تقدمت به الحكومة في جلسة البرلمان امس .

Use the vocabulary that they contain to write one or more Arabic news stories of your own around the following words/phrases:

registered to vote – to cancel elections – to hold early elections – to debate – parliamentary term/session – sitting of parliament – pessimistic

UNIT 7

War

GENERAL REMARKS

This unit uses a minimum of technical vocabulary in exercises designed to develop the following skills:

Lesson 7.1: aural comprehension of, and sustained oral translation into, the comparatively informal Arabic of news features and interviews;

Lesson 7.2: (revision); sustained oral translation into and out of formal Media Arabic;

Lesson 7.3: selective aural information-gathering; quick vocabulary acquisition (with particular reference to complex structures and variants).

The exercises which follow each lesson contain additional vocabulary. They must be completed before moving on the the next lesson and Unit 8.

Note: remember that war (*ḥarb*) is feminine →

اندلعت الحرب ، قاد حربا أهلية ، الحرب الدائرة في جنوب السودان الخ.

LESSON 7.1: INVASION AND SIDE-EFFECTS OF WAR

The exercises in the Classroom Practice deal with invasion and the economic side-effects of war; the Homework exercises deal with military forces and troop movements.

CLASSROOM PRACTICE

7.1.1 Aural/Oral Exercise

(a) Listen to the following passage, which will be read aloud twice by the teacher. Write down any new Arabic terms.

القوات العراقية تغزو الكويت وتسيطر على العاصمة وتحتل قصر الأمير والمراكز الاستراتيجية

صرح مصدر مسئول† في وزارة الدفاع الكويتية بأنه في حوالَي الساعة الثانية من فجر أمس بدأت القوات العراقية احتراق الحدود الشمالية واحتلال عدة مواقع داخل أراضي الكويت.

(b) Translate sentences 1–10 orally into English.

1. Iraqi forces invade Kuwait!
2. Iraq invades Kuwait!
3. Iraq invaded Kuwait early yesterday morning.
4. Iraq invaded Kuwait early yesterday, and Iraqi forces today control the capital.
5. Iraq invaded Kuwait early yesterday, and Iraqi forces now control the capital, the Emir's palace and a number of strategic points.
6. Iraqi forces have crossed the border.
7. Iraqi forces crossed the frontier at about three o'clock this morning and occupied a number of positions on Kuwaiti soil.
8. Israeli forces have crossed the frontiers to the south and north and now control about thirteen towns and villages and other strategic points.
9. The forces of the alliance have crossed the southern and western borders and have taken up position inside Iraq.
10. Insurgent forces have taken control of the capital and a number of other strategic points.

7.1.2 Aural/Written Exercise

Listen to the following sentences, which will be read aloud twice at dictation speed by the teacher. As you listen, write an English translation of the sentences.

†This spelling is incorrect, but frequent in Media Arabic, as are other misspellings involving *hamzah*.

١ـ ذُكر ان القوّات العراقية احتلت المباني الحكومية .

٢ـ ذكر ان القوات العراقية احتلت المباني الحكومية ، بما فيها مبنى وزارة الدفاع .

٣ـ الشعب المصري يقول لا ! للغزْو العراقي !

٤ـ الشارع المصري يقول لا للغزو العراقي لأنه يتم غزو بلد عربي لبلد عربي آخر .

٥ـ قال مواطن مصري : معنى هذا الغزو ان لغة الحوار اصبحت لا معنى لها .

٦ـ تساءل مواطن سعودي : لماذا اصبحت كلمة مفاوضات بلا معنىً في المنطقة؟

٧ـ دعا مواطن كويتي موجود في مصر الى تكوين قوة اسلامية عربية لمواجهة القوات العراقية .

٨ـ قال : الموقف الآن في يد العرب الذين يجب ان يجتمعوا ويقرروا إنهاء هذا الوضع غير المقبول .

٩ـ قال انه ينبغي تكوين قوة اسلامية عربية لمواجهة القوات العراقية إذا اقتضى الأمر ذلك .

١٠ـقال : إذا تدخلت مصر فسوف تتحرك جميع الدول العربية .

7.1.3 *Aural/Written Exercise*

1. Listen to the following passages, which will be read aloud twice at dictation speed by the teacher. Summarise the passages in English.
2. Listen to the same passages being read aloud again, and write them down in Arabic. Compare your versions with the texts below, and discuss any points of difficulty.

تواجه المنطقة العربية والدول النامِيَة أزمة اقتصادية صعبة كنتيجة مباشِرة للغزو العراقي للكويت . فالارتباط الذي كان قائما بين دول المنطقة ، وخصوصا في مجال العَمالة الموجودة في الكويت والعراق ، وفي مجال التبادُل التجاري والمالي ، أدى بعد تطبيق الدول العربية للمقاطعة الاقتصادية ضد العراق الى انعكاسات سلبية على اقتصاديات دول المنطقة ودول العالم الثالث .

al-Majallah, 29 September to 2 October 1990

الحرب اللبنانية غيرت كل شيء في البلاد . غيرت الإنسان والأرض والتقاليد والماء والهواء والسماء كما بدّلت المفاهيم والأخلاق . تغير عيش اللبنانيين فحتى مهنة قيادة السيارات العمومية شملها التغيير . فأصبح سائقو تاكسي بيروت من الضُّبّاط والجامعيين . فالأوضاع المعيشية الراهنة في لبنان صعبة ، الأمر الذي يدفع بالكثيرين من اللبنانيين الى القيام بعمل إضافي الى جانب ما يقومون به من أعمال أصلية . لذلك لا تعجبْ إذا رأيت عسكريين او رجال دين او موظَّفين حكوميين يسوقون سيارات التاكسي في بيروت .

Majallat al-Sharq al-Awasaṭ, 26 October 1990

7.1.4 *Oral Exercise*

Translate the following passage into Arabic, section by section, trying to keep up an even speed with as few hesitations as possible. Repeat the exercise, if necessary, until fluency is achieved.

A: Two days ago, Iraq invaded Kuwait. What are your views, as an Arab, on the current situation in the Gulf? /

B: Some people say it's up to the Arabs now. I think the Arab states have got to act, but if they won't, then America must. /

A: You want America to act; you think the West should intervene. By that, do you mean military intervention? /

B: If necessary. The present situation is unacceptable. It's unacceptable for one country to invade another without any reaction, any intervention, by the international community. /

A: But western military intervention would be unacceptable to most Arab states, wouldn't? Isn't it really up to the Arabs to resolve this crisis themselves? /

B: To resolve a crisis, there has to be a dialogue, and it seems that the concept of dialogue has become totally meaningless among the parties involved. /

A: But negotiations were going on between Iraq and Kuwait prior to the invasion. /

B: And the result of those negotiations was that Iraq decided on military intervention. /

A: Egypt is bound to have an important influence on how things develop in the days and weeks to come. What does the Egyptian public have to say about the Iraqi invasion of Kuwait? /

B: The average Egyptian wants an immediate end to the Iraqi occupation. Several Egyptians have told me that they think their government ought to act, that they wonder why it hasn't acted yet. Of course the Egyptian government is worried about Egyptian citizens still in Iraq. /

A: I wonder why it is that most Palestinians and many Jordanians seem to support Saddam? /

B: Jordan is a developing nation which was already facing an economic crisis before the invasion. The Gulf crisis, and in particular the trade embargo, has made living conditions in Jordan very difficult. And Palestinians support Saddam because Saddam supports Palestinian resistance to the Israeli occupation. /

A: And now Saddam himself is occupying the territory of a sister Arab state. /

B: The Palestinians have been suffering from a great sense of isolation within the Arab community. Many of them feel that Iraq is the only Arab state that has always stood by them, always supported them against Israel. /

A: They consider that fact more important than the repercussions of what Iraq has done on Arab unity? /

B: They certainly consider it more important than what some of them perceive as Arab unity *against* the Palestinians. That, at any rate, is the position held by some extremists. /

A: Of course, Yemen has also declared its support for Iraq. Why is that, do you think? /

B: The Yemenis want an end to Saudi control of the Arab economy, and are in favour of anything which will diminish Saudi political influence in the region. /

A: Of course, Iraq has tried to gain stategic control of the Gulf region before, during the Iran-Iraq war, for example. /

B: Yes; and during the Iran-Iraq war, most of us supported Saddam as Arabs. This time it's different, though. Iraqi control of the Arab Gulf states would mean the collapse of the region's economy. We'd all end up as taxi-drivers.

HOMEWORK

1. Read the following passages, but do not translate them:

ـ الكويت تطلب انسحاب قوات الغزو فوْرا

ـ دعوة اسلامية لوقف العمليات العسكرية وانسحاب القوات العراقية الى الحدود

الأمين العام لمنظمة المؤتمر الاسلامي يدعو الى الوقف الفوري لكل العمليات العسكرية وانسحاب القوات التي قامت بهذه العمليات الى الحدود المعترَف بها دوليا بـين العـراق والكويت .

ـ اعلنت مصر موقفها الرافض للغزو العراقي وطالبت العراق بالجلاء عن الكويت .

ـ سحب الأسلحة النووية الأمريكية من كوريا

قالت وكالة كورية للأنباء امس ان الأسلحة النووية الأمريكية ستُسحب من كوريا الجنوبية هذا العام وان من المتوقع إعلان البلاد منطقة خاليَة من الأسلحة النووية .

Use the vocabulary that they contain to write an Arabic news story of your own around the following words/phrases:

military operations – immediate – to evacuate   to withdraw   nuclear-free

2. Read the following passages, but do not translate them:

ـ قد قدَّرت المصادر الدبلوماسية في الكويت حجم القوة العراقية بـ ٢٠ الف جنديّ .

ـ اكد مسؤولون في وزارة الدفاع الامريكية ما اعلنه وزيرالدفاع من انّ نحو ٢٠ الفا من جنود الجيش والقوات الجوية موجودون الآن في السعودية .

ـ اعلنت وزارة الدفاع الامريكية ان عدد القوات الامريكية في الكويت وجنوبي العراق ارتفع بشكل حادّ ووصل الى ٤٣٠ الف جندي .

ـ عبرت الولايات المتحدة عن استعدادها لإرسال قوات إضافية الى الخليج اذا اقتضى الأمر ذلك .

ـ اكدت الولايات المتحدة استعدادها لإنهاء الاحتلال العراقي للكويت باستخدام القوة العسكرية طِبْقا لِميثاق الأمم المتحدة اذا اقتضى الأمر ذلك .

ـ قد قدرت المصادر الدبلوماسية في الكويت حجم القوة العراقية المهاجمة بــ ٢٠ الف جندي وتقول التقارير ان قوة الهجوم العراقية استولت على قصر الأمير وعلى عدة مراكز استراتيجية .

ـ هاجم المتمرِّدون السودانيون عدة قواعد عسكرية في جنوب البلاد .

ـ تعتبر "جيبوتي" احدى أهم القواعد العسكرية الفرنسية في الخارج .

ـ اوضح متحدث باسم "البنتاجون" ان القوات الاميركية في منطقة الخليج ما زالت تشكل أساسا قوة دفاعية ولكنها قادرة على التحول الى قوة هجومية ضاربة .

ـ اعرب وزير الدولة البريطاني للشؤون الخارجية عن امله بأن تتوصل دول مجلس التعاون الخليجي الى تشكيل قوة رَدْع تابعة لها† .

---

†The force of the phrase *tābi' li-* varies. In an earlier example (page 60), it indicated a relationship of belonging or control: *al-wizārāt al-tābi'ah lahā (li 'l-sharikāt allatī tumawwiluhā 'l-ḥukūmah)*, 'the ministries which control/are in charge of them (= the state-funded companies)/their ministries'. In the present example (*quwwat rad' tābi'ah lahā*), the phrase indicates a relationship of belonging or being controlled, and is used emphatically: 'a deterrent force under their control/their own deterrent force/a deterrent force of their own'. In some subsequent examples (e.g. page 132), the phrase is merely a substitute for an *iḍāfah*: *ṭā'irāt miḥwariyyah tābi'ah lahā (li-Isrā'īl)'* = 'her (= Israel's) helicopters', 'Israeli helicopters'. When used in this way, the phrase may be considered a typical piece of Media Arabic padding. It has a parallel in the colloquial possessive particles *tibā'/bitā'*.

Use the vocabulary that they contain to write one or more Arabic news stories of your own around the following words/phrases:

rebels – military base – air force – attack(ing) force(s) – strike force – defence force – deterrent force – the Charter of the United Nations – to estimate – to be prepared/ready

3. Read the following passages, but do not translate them.

ـ قد قدرت المصادر الدبلوماسية في الكويت حجم القوة العراقية بـ ٢٠ الف جندي وتقود هذه القوات وَحْدات من الحرس الجمهوري العراقي .

ـ العراق يحشد ٤٣٠ الف جندي على الحدود مع السعودية

ـ جنّد العراقيون كل من هو قادر على حمل السلاح حتى سن الخامسة والستين .

ـ واشنطن تستدعي ٢٢ الف من الحرس الوطني والاحتياط لتعزيز قواتها بالخليج

ـ قال وزير الدفاع الامريكي ان اكثر من ١٠٠ الف عسكري امريكي منتشرون في الخليج وان المزيد في طريقهم الى هناك . وقال ان الانتشار لم ينته بعدُ وان اي قرار لم يتخذ بالنسبة الى الحجم النهائي لهذا الانتشار .

ـ اكد مسؤول في وزارة الدفاع الاميركية ما اعلنه وزير الدفاع من ان نحو ١٠٠ الف من مُشاة البحرية الاميركية وجنود الجيش والقوات الجوية موجودون الآن في السعودية . وقال المسؤولون : هذا العدد لا يشمل نحو ٢٥ الفا من البحّارة والطيّارين على مَتْنِ نحو ٤٠ سفينة حربية في الخليج والبحر الأحمر وخليج عمان وشرق البحر المتوسط .

ـ قام مشاة البحرية الامريكية وبحارة من السِّرْب الثاني البرمائي ووحدة مشاة البحرية الثانية والعشرين امس بمناورات مشتركة مع القوات الكويتية .

(a) Briefly explain the derivation of the following terms:

اسْتَدْعَى ـ احتياط ـ البحرية ـ مُشاة البحرية ـ سِرْب

(b) Write one or more Arabic news stories of your own around the following words/phrases:

to draft – conscript – to call up – to mass – to be deployed – reserve – unit – squadron – soldier – sailor – marine – airborne troops – on board (a ship/aircraft)

*4. Tape
This lesson's broadcast contains two news stories. Transcribe both stories in Arabic, and translate them into idiomatic English. Make brief notes on any linguistic features that you think deserve comment.

LESSON 7.2: TROOPS AND MILITARY HARDWARE

The exercises in the Classroom Practice are revision exercises which consolidate the vocabulary learnt in Lesson 7.1 and apply it to journalistic story-structures familiar from Part I; the Homework exercises deal with military hardware.

CLASSROOM PRACTICE

7.2.1 Oral Exercise

Translate the following passage into Arabic orally, section by section. Repeat the exercise, if necessary, until fluency is achieved.

During his visit yesterday to American trooops stationed in Saudi Arabia, President Bush said that the USA was ready for war, / and once more called upon Iraqi forces to withdraw to the internationally-recognised boundary between Kuwait and Iraq. / The number of American troops stationed in Saudi Arabia is now estimated at 200,000, / not including some 35,000 marines and airborne troops now on their way to the Gulf from the eastern Mediterranean on board some forty American warships. / Washington is calling up reservists to reinforce troops already in the Gulf; a British military force arrived in Saudi Arabia some weeks ago, / and some Arab states, including Egypt, have already sent troops and military experts to the region. / Syria announced yesterday that it was ready to send troops to the Gulf if necessary. / The number of Iraqi troops deployed in Kuwait is unknown. / When Iraq invaded Kuwait on 2 August, foreign observers estimated the strength of Iraqi forces at some 35,000. / Since then, the number of Iraqi soldiers deployed in Kuwait itself and in southern Iraq has risen sharply. / It is known that Iraq has reinforced the units of the Republican Guard which spearheaded the attack on Kuwait City with extra troops from the Iran-Iraq border. / These extra troops are essentially a defensive force, but are capable of becoming a strike force. / Many Kuwaitis and most foreign residents have now evacuated Kuwait, / though a number of foreign workers remain in Baghdad and in a number of other Iraqi cities and military bases. /

The repercussions of the current situation in the Gulf are both political and economic. / On the political front, the Islamic Congress has called for an immediate end to all military operations and the withdrawal of Iraqi troops to the internationally-recognised frontier, / but not all Arab states condemn the Iraqi invasion, although the majority of Muslim states support the call for an Iraqi withdrawal. / In Europe, only Britain has shown complete support for American policy in the Gulf, / and the Soviet Union, which still has large numbers of military experts in Iraq, is still trying to bring about a peaceful solution to the crisis through negotiation and dialogue.

7.2.2 Oral Exercise

Listen to the following passage, which will be read aloud once by the teacher. It will then be read aloud section by section for you to translate orally into English. Guess the meaning of any unfamiliar terms.

توجه امس يفغني بريماكوف مبعوث الرئيس السوفياتي ميخائيل غورباتشوف الى دمشق من القاهرة وأجرى محادثات مع الرئيس حافظ الأسد تناولت أزمة الخليج ./ ويتوقع ان يعود بريماكوف الى القاهرة لمقابلة الرئيس حسني مبارك وان ينتقل مساء اليوم او غدا الى جدة لإجراء محادثات مع كبار المسؤولين السعوديين على رأسهم الملك فهد بن عبد العزيز ./

وفي تطور آخر تلقى الملك امس مكالمة هاتفية من الرئيس الاميركي جورج بوش واستعرضا خلالها الأوضاع الراهنة في المنطقة ./ وقد اعلن امس وزير الدفاع الاميركي ريتشارد تشيني ان بلاده تنوي زيادة عدد قواتها الموجودة في منطقة الخليج بنحو ١٠٠ الف رجل ./

وأجرى الرئيس المصري محادثات مع السلطان قابوس بن سعيد، وصرح لدى وصوله الى مسقط بأن "قيادة دول الخليج سيدرسون الموقف ويقوّمونه في ما بينهم / في ما يخص المستقبل بعد حل أزمة الخليج لإيجاد نظام دفاع عربي ـ عربي لحماية المنطقة من أية أخطار مستقبلية"./ وأضاف الرئيس مبارك ان الدول الاجنبية يجب "ألا تساعد إلا في ما يطلب منها من سلاح" / مشيرا الى انه ابلغ قيادة دول الخليج التي زارها ان مصر "على اتم الاستعداد للتعاون معهم في ما يصلون اليه من تصور للدفاع عن المنطقة". وعاد الرئيس المصري مساء الى القاهرة ولم يدل بأي تصريحات ./

ومن واشنطن يكتب مراسل "الحياة" ان وزير الدفاع الاميركي ريتشارد تشيني اعلن ان الولايات المتحدة لم تصل حتى الآن الى النقطة التي ستوقف فيها ارسال القوات الاميركية الى منطقة الخليج، / ولم يستبعد ان تزيد عدد قواتها هناك نحو ١٠٠ الف جندي آخر ./ واضاف تشيني الذي كان يتحدث في سلسلة من المقابلات التلفزيونية امس ان الادارة لم تضع منذ البداية حدا أقصى لعدد القوات الاميركية في المنطقة / و "ان السؤال هو متى

سنوقف إرسال القوات والجواب اننا لم نصل الى النقطة التي سنوقف فيها ارسال القوات". / وتوقع استمرار إرسال القوات في المرحلة المقبلة لأسباب عدة أبرزها "إبقاء خيارات الحل العسكري مفتوحة" اذا قرر الرئيس بوش ذلك . /

وقال تشيتي "لم نُسقط أيا من الخيارات". / واوضح تشيني الذي كان عقد و†وزير الخارجية جيمس بيكر مساء الاربعاء اجتماعا مغلقا مع زعماء الكونغرس للبحث في أزمة الخليج ان العراق لا يزال ينشر مزيدا من القوات في الكويت / ولديه الكثير من المدرّعات الثقيلة التي يمكنها إمّا شنّ هجوم في اتجاه الجنوب وإمّا البقاء في الكويت ./ وقدر تشيني عدد القوات العراقية الموجودة في مَسْرح العمليات الكويتية بنحو ٤٠٠ الف جندي . /

وأشار الى ان عدد القوات الاميركية في منطقة الخليج مرتبط بتطورات الوضع هناك ./ واوضح ان القوات الاميركية في المنطقة هي الآن في وضع استعداد "للردع والدفاع ولتنفيذ العقوبات الاقتصادية ضد العراق". / لكنه شدد على ان المطلوب ان تكون القوات الاميركية مستعدة لكل الاحتمالات .

al-Ḥayāh, 26 October 1990

7.2.3 *Oral Exercise*

Listen to the following passage, which will be read aloud, section by section, by the teacher. Orally, translate it into idiomatic English, guessing the meaning of unfamiliar terms and omitting inessentials. Try to keep up an even speed, with as few hesitations as possible. Repeat the exercise, if necessary, until fluency is achieved.

يغادر وزيرالخارجية الامريكي جيمس بيكر واشنطن اليوم متوجها الى الشرق الاوسط واوروبا في جولة اكدت المصادر السياسية والدبلوماسية في العاصمة الامريكية انها ستكون كبيرة الاهمية في المرحلة الراهنة سواء بالنسبة للولايات المتحدة نفسها او بالنسبة لتطورات أزمة الخليج ./ ومن المقرر ان تبدأ جولة بيكر بزيارة للبحرين ثم يتوجه الى السعودية فمصر قبل ان يستأنف جولته التي تشمل تركيا وعددا من العواصم الاوروبية حيث ينتظر ان يجتمع في احداها مع وزير الخارجية السوفييتي ./

---

†This is the '*wāw* of accompaniment', which takes the accusative and may be substituted for *ma'a*. It occurs sporadically in Media Arabic, and should not be mistaken for a misprint.

وذكرت صحيفة واشنطن بوست امس ان الهدف الرئيسي من جولة بيكر هو دعم التحالف القائم وتنسيق التعاون بين القوات المنتشرة في الجزيرة والخليج . / وقالت ان الجولة تأتي في وقت دُقّت فيه طبول الحرب وازداد فيه التوتّر داخل الولايات المتحدة وخارجها . / واكدت الصحيفة ان أزمة الخليج تتحرك الآن الى ما يبدو انه سيكون مرحلة دقيقة وقالت ان جيمس بيكر يُدْرِك ان مخاطر هذه المرحلة ستكون كبيرة . /

وعلى نفس الصعيد أذاع راديو صوت امريكا امس ان حاملة الطائرات الامريكية "ميدواي" وصلت الى منطقة الخليج وهي رابع حاملة طائرات في المنطقة . / وقال الراديو ان وزارة الدفاع الامريكية لم تعلن ما اذا كانت حاملة الطائرات "ميدواي" ستحل محل حاملة طائرات أخرى او ان الحاملات الاربع ستبقى في المنطقة . / وأورد الراديو ـ من جهة أخرى ـ تصريحات أدلى بها الجنرال نورمان شوارتزكوف قائد القوات الامريكية في الخليج لصحيفة "نيو يورك تايمز" امس وقال فيها ان بوسْع القوات الامريكية تدمير العراق واضاف شوارتزكوف ان الحرب يمكن ان تندلع في اي وقت . /

على نفس الصعيد استنكر ادوارد هيث رئيس وزراء بريطانيا الاسبق تصريحات الرئيس الامريكي عن العراق والتي أشار فيها الى ان صبره نَفِدَ . / وقال هيث في حديث على شاشات تلفزيون هيئة الاذاعة البريطانية اذيع اول امس ان ما يجب عمله في الشرق الاوسط هو حل مشكلة تتطلب بذل جهود دبلوماسية كبيرة وهذه الجهود لم تبذل . /

من ناحية أخرى هاجم وزير الخارجية الفرنسي الاسبق الرئيس بوش لموقفه من العراق وقال انه داعية حرب على ما يبدو . / وقال الرئيس الفرنسي فرانسو ميتران في حديث نُشر امس بالقاهرة ان الأمر الجوهري في أزمة الخليج هو احترام القانون الذي ينتفي بدونه النظام الدولي . / و لكنه اكد وهو يشير الى النزاع العربي الاسرائيلي والقضية اللبنانية ان قواعد القانون التي يجب احترامها فيما يتعلق بأزمة الخليج ينبغي ان تحترم ايضا في جميع أنحاء العالم تطبيقا لقرارات الامم المتحدة . /

ومن جهة أخرى اكد أحمد عيسى سفير سوريا في تونس ان الدعوة الى عقد قمة عربية في الظروف الراهنة أمر لا يفيد ./ وقال انه لو انسحب العراق من الكويت لتولدت ظروف جديدة تستحق الدراسة ./ واضاف في حديث ادلى به لصحيفة "الصباح" التونسية امس ان موقف سوريا من أزمة الخليج لم يتغير وهي حريصة منذ البداية على سلامة الجيش العراقي والشعب العراقي ./ وحذر الأمير حسن ولي عهد الاردن من خطورة أزمة الخليج ونقلت صحيفة "تايمز" البريطانية قلقه تُجاهَ الوضع الراهن ../ وقالت الصحيفة نقلا عن الامير حسن ان الفرصة الوحيدة لمنع الحرب تتمثل في تجدد محاولات الحل السلمي من جانب العرب والمجتمع الدولي مشيرا في ذلك الصدد الى جولة العاهل الاردني الحالية والتي تشمل عددا من الدول الاوروبية ./

ومن ناحية أخرى تسلم الرئيس الايراني علي أكبر هاشمي رفسنجاني رسالة خطية من رئيس وزراء اليابان تتعلق بتطورات الاوضاع في منطقة الخليج وعدد من القضايا الدولية ذات الاهتمام المشترك اضافة الى العلاقات بين البلدين ./ على صعيد آخر عقدت في طهران مساء امس جلسة مباحثات بين الدكتور علي أكبر ولايتي وزير خارجية ايران والدكتور حامد الغابد الامين العام لمنظمة المؤتمر الاسلامي الذي يزور طهران حاليا . وذكر راديو طهران ان المباحثات تناولت قضايا العالم الاسلامي ./ واختتمت في عمان اول امس اجتماعات كبار الخبراء والمسئولين في اللجنة الاقتصادية لغربي آسيا التابعة للأمم المتحدة وقال الامين العام التنفيذي للجنة انه تم خلال الاجتماعات اجراء دراسات حول الانعكاسات السلبية لأزمة الخليج على اقتصاد دول المنطقة .

al-Thawrah (Yemen), 3 November 1990

HOMEWORK

1. Write an Arabic news story of your own around the following words/ phrases:

to evaluate – to rule out an option – to apply economic sanctions – to emphasise – field of operations / theatre of war

2. Write one or more Arabic news stories of your own around the following words/phrases:

war propaganda – sabre-rattling – tension – essential – safety – aircraft carrier – to be in someone's power to … to take the place of – to resume/recommence – to destroy – to quote someone as saying – new circumstances will arise

3. Read the following passages, but do not translate them.

ـ القوات العراقية تغزو الكويت وتسيطر على العاصمة وتحتل قصر الأمير

عملية الغزو بدأت فجر أمس بواسطة الدبّابات وتحت غطاء جوي ٣٥٠ دبّابة انتشرت في الغزو.

قد قدرت المصادر الدبلوماسية في الكويت حجم القوة العراقية المهاجمة بـ ٣٥٠ دبّابة ، وتقود هذه القوات وحدات الحرس الجمهوري العراقي .

ـ هاجم مجهولون ليلة أمس مقهيين في "جيبوتي" بثلاث قنابل يدوية مما أدى الى مقتل فتيً فرنسي. وبدا ان الهجوم الذي وقع ليل الخميس – الجمعة استهدف الجنود الفرنسيين في "جيبوتي" التي تعتبر احدى اهم القواعد العسكرية الفرنسية في الخارج. وقال شهود العيان ان قنبلتين لم تنفجرا في حين انفجرت القنبلة الثالثة. وقد أدان المتحدث باسم وزارة الخارجية الفرنسية الهجوم وقال ان اغتيال طفل يعدّ جريمة بَشِعَة .

ـ اعلنت وزارة الدفاع الامريكية ان عدد القوات العراقية في الكويت و جنوبي العراق ارتفع بشكل حاد ليصل الى ٤٣٠ الف جندي وذلك إضافة الى ٣٥٠٠ دبابة و ٢٢٠٠ ناقلة جنود مدرَّعة و ١٧٠٠ قطْعَة مدفْعية. وهذا يعني ان العراق عزز قواته بـ ١٦٥ الف جنديَ خلالَ اسبوعين فقط وهو ما يماثل تقريبا عدد القوات الامريكية التي انتشرت بالخليج طوالَ الاسابيع السبعة الماضية .

ـ قتل الجنرال في الجيش الافغاني علاء الدين عندما انفجر **لغم** بسيارته في أثناء تفقّده مواقع عسكرية قبل يومين في "هلمند" **جنوبي غربي** افغانستان. وبهذا يكون عدد الجنرالات الذين قتلوا خلال الاسبوع الماضي ثلاثة .

ـ هاجمت القوات الاسرائيلية امس عدة قرى و**مخيّمات** في الجنوب اللبناني بـ <u>القَصْف المِدْفعي</u> و <u>الصاروخي</u> .

ـ اعلنت الولايات المتحدة انها بدأت بـ<u>نشر</u> <u>صواريخ</u> "باتريوت" المضادّة للصواريخ في منطقة الخليج .

Use the words/phrases underlined to write one or more Arabic news stories of your own around the following words/phrases:

to the south of – south-west of – (refugee) camp – to be equivalent to – rocket – rocket and artillery fire – to deploy – to inspect – (piece of) artillery – armoured personnel carrier – tank – hand-grenade – to explode – air cover – murder – eye-witness – mine

*4. Tape

This lesson's broadcast contains three news stories. Transcribe the first two stories and translate them into idiomatic English. Summarise the third story in English. Make brief notes on any linguistic features that you think deserve comment.

LESSON 7.3: MILITARY ENGAGEMENTS; CASUALTIES

The exercises in the Classroom Practice deal with military engagements, terrorist attacks, casualties and prisoners; the Homework exercises consolidate the vocabulary learnt during Classroom Practice.

CLASSROOM PRACTICE

7.3.1 Aural/Written Exercise

1. Listen to the following passages, which will each be read aloud twice by the teacher, and in each case, in writing, identify the type of attack described (e.g. air or land attack, shelling or grenades, etc.). Ignore any other information.

2. Compare your notes with the texts below and discuss any points of difficulty.

١ـ أسفر استئناف القصف المدفعي والصاروخي في الجنوب اللبناني في الايام الثلاثة الماضية عن سقوط اكثر من ٣٥ قتيلا و ٢٠٠ جريح .

٢ـ أعادت الجامعة الامريكية في بيروت فتح أبوابها أمس واستأنفت الدراسة في جميع الصفوف بعد ثلاثة ايام على انفجار سيارة ملغومة دمّرت مبناها الرئيسي .

٣ـ واصلت اسرائيل هجوماتها على الجنوب اللبناني بالقصف المدفعي والجوي وشنّت طائرات مروحية تابعة لها† غارات على مدينة النبطية أصابت خلالها مقرّ المكتب السياسي لـ "حزب الله" في المدينة . وأدت عملية القصف الى سقوط عدد من الضحايا وتدمير كثير من المنازل .

٤ـ اعترفت وزارة الحربية الامريكية ان القوات الامريكية في اليوم الاول من الهجوم البَرّي على القوات العراقية دفنت جنودا عراقيين أحياء بواسطة دبابات وجَرّافات . وأكد متحدث باسم وزارة الحربية الامريكية انه "ليست هناك طريقة مستحَبّة للقتل في زمن الحرب" وأضاف ان "الحرب هي الجحيم" .

†See the footnote on page 122.

7.3.2 Reading Exercise

Silently read the two following groups of passages, and quickly assimilate
the terms/constructions underlined.

● **Attacks**

ـ هجوم مسلّح على الجنود الفرنسيين في جيبوتي

شنّت جماعات إرهابية يعتقد انها مؤيدة للعراق **هجوما** إرهابيا
على مقهيين في جيبوتي امس .

ـ **شنّت** جماعات إرهابية يعتقد انها مؤيدة للعراق **هجوما** إرهابيا
على مقهيين في جيبوتي امس .

ـ واصلت اسرائيل **اعتداءاتها على** الجنوب اللبناني بالقصف
المدفعي و **شنّت** طائرات مروحية تابعة لها **غارات على** مدينة
النبطية . وأدت **عمليات القصف** الى سقوط عدد من الضحايا .

● **Casualties**

ـ **قُتل** الجنرال في الجيش الافغاني علاء الدين عندما انفجر لغم
بسيارته امس . وبهذا يكون عدد **الجنرالات الذين قُتلوا خلال
الاسبوع** ثلاثة .

ـ هاجم مجهولون مقهيين في جيبوتي بثلاث قنابل يدوية
مِمّا أدّى الى مَقْتَل فتىً فرنسي .

ـ أدّت عمليات القصف الى **سقوط** عدد من **الضحايا** .

ـ **أسْفَرت** معاودة القصف المدفعي والصاروخي **عن** سقوط اكثر
من ٣٥ **قتيلا** و ٢٠٠ جريح .

ـ أسفر الهجوم الإرهابي عن إصابة ١٦ فرنسيا بجروح خطيرة .

ـ أسْفر الهجوم المسلح عن إصابة ١٦ فرنسيا بـجروح طفيفة .

7.3.3 *Aural/Written Exercise*

1. Listen to the following passages, which will each be read aloud twice by the teacher, and in each case, in writing, identify the type of attack and the number and type of casualties.
2. Compare your notes with the texts below, and discuss any points of difficulty.

١ـ قتل جنرالان في الجيش الافغاني عندما انفجرت ألغام بسيارتهما امس وبهذا يكون عدد الجنرالات الذين قتلوا خلال الاسبوع تسعة .

٢ـ واصلت اسرائيل اعتداءاتها على الجنوب اللبناني بالقصف المدفعي والجوي وشنت طائرات هليكوبتر تابعة لها غارات على مدينة النبطية أصابت خلالها مقر المكتب السياسي لـ "حزب الله" في المدينة . وأسفرت عمليات القصف عن سقوط ٩ ضحايا وتدمير ٨ منازل .

٣ـ في هجوم إرهابي هاجم مجهولان ليلة امس مقهيً في جيبوتي مما أسفر عن مقتل صبي فرنسي وسقوط ٧ جَرْحى و ٥ قَتْلى من المواطنين الجيبوتيين .

٤ـ أدى هجوم بتسع قنابل يدوية على مقهىً في جيبوتي الى مقتل فتىً فرنسي وإصابة ٣٩ فرنسيا بجروح طفيفة إضافة الى مواطن جيبوتي نُقل الى المستشفى في حال الخطر الشديد .

٥ـ شنت جماعات إرهابية هجوما بالقنابل على ثلاثة مقاهٍ في جيبوتي مما أدى الى مَصْرَع فتاة فرنسية وإصابة ١٧ جنديا بجروح خطيرة . وقد أدان متحدث باسم وزارة الخارجية الفرنسية الهجوم وقال ان اغتيال طفلة يعد جريمة بشعة .

٦ـ قال بيان عسكري امريكي امس ان ضابطين من مشاة البحرية نقلا الى المستشفى لإصابتهما بجروح طفيفة بعد انفجار لغم بسيارتهما .

7.3.4 Reading Exercise

Silently read the two following groups of passages, and quickly assimilate the terms/constructions underlined.

● **Military movements**

ـ فرضت الحكومة اللبنانية ابتداءً من فجر امس حصاراً على المناطق الخاضعة لسيطرة العماد ميشل عون ومنعت السيارات من دخولها .

ـ صرح احد قادة التمرد على زعيم "الحركة الشعبية لتحرير السودان" العقيد جون قرنق بأن قواته تسيطر على عدة مراكز استراتيجية في جنوب السودان وقال انه طلب من جون قرنق الاستسلام .

ـ انهار وقف إطلاق النار الذي كان سائداً وعاد الاقتتال مجددا الى الجنوب السوداني في محاولة من كل طرف الى تعزيز موقفه .

● **Prisoners**

ـ يحاول ممثلو القيادة الروسية إيجاد حل لمسألة الإفراج عن الأسرى الروس لدى المجاهدين الافغان .

ـ يذكر ان العراق والكويت مختلفان حول عدد المحتجَزين الكويتيين في العراق. وفي الوقت الذي تؤكد فيه بغداد انها تحتجز ٣٥٧٦ أسيراً كويتيا تطالب الكويت بعودة ٢٤٤٣ شخصا فقط .

7.3.5 *Aural/Written Exercise*

The following two sets of passages will be read out by the teacher as if taken from a broadcast news bulletin (headlines followed by detailed reports); the two sequences will be read aloud consecutively three times. They contain both items from this lesson's vocabulary and variants of familiar items.

1. Translate the headlines into written English.
2. Attempt to summarise the detailed reports in writing in English, concentrating on figures and familiar vocabulary and ignoring other information.
3. Compare your summaries with the texts below, and discuss any points of difficulty.

ـ مقتل طالبين في انفجار في جامعة يابانية

ـ مقتل سائحة المانية بالقدس الشريف

ـ تبادل أسرى بين العراق وايران

ـ مقتل ١٣ شخصا في كشمير في اشتباكات بين المتشددين الكشميريين والشرطة الهندية

ـ صحيفة عراقية توجه تحذيرا الى المعارضين العراقيين وتدعوهم الى الاستسلام

١ـ ذكر مسؤول من إدارة مكافحة الحرائق اليابانية ان انفجارا كبيرا وقع في معمل في جامعة اوساكا وسط اليابان امس مما أسفر عن مقتل طالبين وإصابة ثلاثة آخرين بجروح . وقال المسؤول ان الانفجار أدى الى حريق دمر المعمل حيث كان الطلبة يقومون بتجربة في الهندسة الكهربائية بالجامعة الواقعة على بعد ٤٠٠ كيلومتر غربي طوكيو . ولم يتم التوصل الى أسباب الانفجار .

٢ـ أعلن ناطق باسم الشرطة الاسرائيلية ان سائحة قتلت وجرحت اثنتان أخريان طَعْنا بالسكاكين بعد ظهر امس في مدينة القدس القديمة . وأوضح الناطق ان السائحة المتوفّاة وكذلك جريحة أخرى تحملان الجِنْسية الالمانية .

٣ـ اعلن العراق انه سيُفرج عن ٢٣٩ أسيرا ايرانيا لديه ابتداء من يوم الاربعاء المقبل . ونقلت وكالة الأنباء العراقية عن ناطق رسمي في الخارجية العراقية ان إطلاق سراح هؤلاء الأسرى تم الاتفاق عليه خلال زيارة الدكتور علي أكبر ولايتي وزير خارجية ايران لبغداد الاسبوع الماضي ومباحثاته مع المسؤولين العراقيين . وتوقع الناطق ان تُطلق ايران بالمقابل سراح ٧٩ أسيرا عراقيا مشيرا الى ان ايران وعدت بإطلاق ٢٠٠ أسير عراقي يوميا اعتبارا من يوم الخميس القادم .

٤ـ قالت الشرطة الهندية ان ١٣ شخصا على الاقل قتلوا محاصَرين أثناء تبادل اطلاق النيران امس إثرَ اشتباكات بين قوات الامن الهندية والمتشددين الكشميريين . وقالت الشرطة ان سبعة اشخاص قتلوا في تبادل لاطلاق النار كما قتلت سيدة إثر انفجار قنبلة يدوية القيت على قوات الامن.

٥ـ الاستسلام او الموت هو الخيار الذي أتاحته صحيفة "بابل" العراقية للثوار العراقيين الذين يعيشون في المَنْفى. قالت الصحيفة ، التي يملكها عُدَيّ ، الابن الأكبر للرئيس صدام حسين، في افتتاحيتها اليوم "ان الشيطان غرر بالمنشقين العراقيين في المَنْفى لكن قد يُغْفَر لهم اذا تابوا وعادوا مرة اخرى الى العراق". وقالت الصحيفة "ان المنشقين سيواجهون الموت اذا استمروا في تآمر ضد صدام".

HOMEWORK

1. Write one or more Arabic news stories of your own around the following words/phrases:

to destroy – to carry out/mount a raid – shelling (operations) – to acknowledge – land/ground attack/offensive – to bury alive – bulldozer – 'there's no nice way of killing people'

2. Write one or more Arabic news stories of your own around the following words/phrases:

terrorist attack – to kill – to wound slightly – to wound seriously – to be taken to hospital in a serious condition – this brings the number of killed and wounded to …

3. (a) Write one or more Arabic news stories of your own around the following words/phrases:

to besiege/surround – to be surrounded and killed – the areas under the control of/controlled by – to surrender – ceasefire – to fire on/shoot – to knife – to hold (prisoners, etc.) – to release (prisoners, etc.) – clashes – exile – editorial (noun) – dissident – to plot against

(b) Use the following words/phrases in one or more complete Arabic sentences of your own:

أَتَاحَ ـ مِن اعتباراً ـ مِن ابِتداءٌ ـ جِنْسية ـ وَقَعَ

*4. Tape
This lesson's broadcast contains three news stories. Transcribe the first two stories and translate them into idiomatic English. Summarise the third story in English. Make brief notes on any linguistic features that you thaink deserve comment.

Law and Order

GENERAL REMARKS

This unit deals briefly with strikes, demonstrations and crime in exercises designed to develop further techniques of aural information-gathering and vocabulary acquisition.

LESSON 8.1: STRIKES, DEMONSTRATIONS AND CRIME

CLASSROOM PRACTICE

8.1.1 Reading Exercise

Silently read the two following groups of passages, and quickly assimilate the terms/constructions underlined.

● **Strikes and demonstrations**

ـ قتل ٢٥ شخصا على الأقل في اشتباكات بـين المواطنـين وقوات الحكومة في مدينة فاس المغربية التي شهدت إضرابا عامًا دعت اليه الاتحادات النقابية للمطالبة بزيادة الأجور .

ـ النقابات الروسية تهدد بإضراب عام احتجاجا على تدهور مستوى المعيشة

ـ نظّم الف طالب تظاهرا امس في اربد (٨٠ كلم شمال عمان) تأييدا لمؤتمر مدريد في حين دعا الاسلاميون الاردنيون الى إضراب احتجاجا على المؤتمر في جامعة عمان يوم افتتاح مؤتمر السلام .

● **Prisoners and processes of law**

ـ اسرائيل تعتقل السوريين في الجولان في عملية ارهابية جديدة في عملية إرهابية جديدة ألقت السلطات الاسرائيلية القَبْضَ على العديد من المواطنين السوريين دون توجيه اتهامات ضدهم .

ـ قررت السلطات الاسرائيلية إبعاد أربعة من مواطني غزة بتُهَم الانتماء الى منظمة "حماس" واتهمتهم بالقيام بعمليات ضد قوات الاحتلال .

ـ القضاء الفرنسي يطلب اعتقال وطرْد مسؤولين ليبيين اتهمهم بـ التورّط في تفجير طائرة فرنسية فوق النيجر

ـ ايران تُعدم ٢٠ مهرُّباً للمخدُّرات

نفّذت **محكمة** ايرانية امس **أحكاما بالإعدام** في ٢٠ شخصا **أُدينوا بـ** تُهمة تهريب المخدرِّات وقتل جنود .

8.1.2 Aural/Written Exercise

Listen to the following passages, which will each be read aloud twice by the teacher.

1. Without taking notes, summarise the passages in English.
2. Compare your summaries with the texts below, and discuss any point of difficulty.

١ـ كشفت الحكومة التشادية الجديدة ان الرئيس السابق حسين حبري قتل جميع السُّجناء السياسيين المعتقلين في سجن خاص داخل القصر الرئاسي وذلك قبل فراره الى الكاميرون .

٢ـ اتهمت الحكومة السودانية الأحزاب السياسية التي حلتها قبل ١٦ شهرا بأنها تقف وراء إضراب نفذه عمال السكك الحديد السودانية .

٣ـ تتكشف مع مرور الايام حقائق جديدة حول العدوان الامريكي على العراق والجرائم التي ارتكبتها القوات المتحالفة خلال هذه الحرب . وهكذا اعترفت وزارة الحربية الامريكية ان القوات الامريكية دفنت جنودا عراقيين أحياء بواسطة دبابات وجرافات .

8.1.3 Aural/Written Exercise

Listen to the following passages, which will each be read aloud twice by the teacher.

1. Make a note of any unfamiliar terms and guess their meaning.
2. Translate the passages orally, explaining how you worked out the meanings of unfamiliar terms.

١ـ اطلقت السلطات الفرنسية سراح عدد من المعتقلين، بينهم فرنسيون ولبنانيون ومغاربة ، ألقي القبض عليهم أثناء زيارة الرئيس اللبناني الياس الهراوي الى باريس بتهمة محاولة الإساءة على الموكب الرسمي للرئيس اللبناني . وذكرت مصادر الشرطة الفرنسية ان بضع عشرات من الشُّبّان والشّابّات قذفوا سيارة الرئيس بالبيض والطماطم غير ان رجال الشرطة ألقوا القبض عليهم .

٢ـ افاد مصدر رسمي بالرباط ان ابراهيم سرفاتي المحكوم عليه بالسجن المؤبّد بتهمة إلماس بالأمن الداخلي والخارجي للدولة تم طرده صباح امس من المغرب . وقد عللت السلطات المغربية طردها للسفراتي بأنه من جنسية برازيلية .

٣ـ وضعت الشرطة الاسرائيلية امس كل وحداتها في حال تأهّب قُصْوى غداة مقتل مستوطنين اسرائيليين بالرُصاص وجرح خمسة آخرين . واعلن كل من "الجبهة الشعبية لتحرير فلسطين" ومنظمة "حزب الله" مسؤوليته عن العملية . وادانت ادارة الرئيس بيل كلينتون الحادث ووصفه بأنه "جريمة بشعة وعمل عنف لا معنى له".

8.1.4 *Aural/Written Exercise*

1. Listen to the following passages, which will each be read aloud twice by the teacher. Write a summary of each passage in English. Adopt whatever method you wish: listening only; listening + notes; transcribing parts or the whole of the Arabic text.
2. Compare your summaries with the texts below, and discuss any points of difficulty.

١ـ النقابات الروسية تهدد بإضراب عام احتجاجا على تدهور مستوى المعيشة

طوّق المتظاهرون مبنى البرلمان الروسي احتجاجا على تدهور الاوضاع الاقتصادية امس . وكان نحو ٥٠ الف متظاهر اجتمعوا في وسط العاصمة استجابة لنداء اتحاد النقابات الذي طالب رئيسه بـ" استقالة الحكّام الذين فَشِلوا في مهمّتهم" وهي "الاصلاح الاقتصادي".

٢ـ ازدادت الاجراءات الامنية المصاحبة لتحركات الرئيس الايراني هاشمي رفسنجاني خلال القمة الاسلامية بعد ان هاجمته سيدتان تردد انهما ايرانيتان .

٣ـ اكدت مصادر مغربية امس الافراج عن عدد من العسكريين الذين ادينوا في العامين ١٩٧١ و ١٩٧٢ بتهم محاولة قَلْب النظام . وقالت مصادر مغربية مسؤولة ان جميع العسكريين المعتقلين سيطلقون قريبا، في اول اشارة الى اعتراف السلطات المغربية

بوجودهم. ويذكر ان محاكم عسكرية اصدرت احكاما بالسجن على مجموعات من العسكريين الذين تورطوا في محاولتين انقلابيتين. الى ذلك اكد الملك الحسن الثاني ان قضايا احترام حقوق الانسان في البلاد ستعرف قريبا طفرة نوعية "تحول المغرب الى مضرب مثل في هذا الشأن".

8.1.5 *Aural/Written Exercise*

Listen to the following passage, which will be read aloud, at moderate speed, once only, by the teacher. It contains vocabulary relating to crime and punishment.

1. Write down the passage in Arabic and summarise it in English.
2. Compare your summaries with the text below, and discuss any points of difficulty.

صنعاء : الشرطة تلقي القبض على شبكة من لصوص المنازل وتستعيد ٢٧ سيارة مسروقة

القت سلطات البحث الجنائي خلال الاسبوع الماضي القبض على عصابة من اللصوص المتخصصين بسرقة المنازل وعدد من المتخصصين في سرقات السيارات . وقال الاخ الدكتور مقدم عمر عبد الكريم مدير عام البحث الجنائي في تصريح للصحف اليمنية "انه قد تم القبض على شبكة من لصوص المنازل تتألف من ١٣ شخصا جميعهم في سن الدراسة الثانوية ويشاركهم موظف حكومي كوسيط لبيع المسروقات التي شملت الأجهزة الكهربائية والأدوات المنزلية وغير ذلك مما تقع عليه ايديهم داخل المنازل". واوضح الاخ مدير عام البحث الجنائي انه تبين ان المهتمّين ليسوا من ذوي السوابق . وقد تم تشكيل لجنة لدراسة الدوافع والاسباب التي ادت الى انحرافهم وجعلتهم يسلكون هذا المسلك . واشار مدير عام البحث الجنائي الى اهمية ان تتلقى هذه القضايا الاهتمام من قِبَل المحاكم وذلك من خلال تشديد العقوبة على المُجرمين ، وفي نفسِ الوقت الاهتمام بهم ورعايتهم إن كانوا أحداثاً . ودعا الى دراسة اوضاع مثل هذه الحالات وايجاد فرص عمل للسَّجين بعد خروجه من السجن حتى لا يعود مجددا لارتكاب جرائم السرقة . من ناحية اخرى ذكر الاخ الدكتور مقدم عمر عبد الكريم بأنه قد تم إلقاء القبض على عدد من سارقي السيارات واكد انه قد تمت

استعادة ٢٧ سيارة مسروقة خلال هذا الشهر . واكد ان ادارة البحث
الجنائي تعمل الآن على انهاء سرقات اطارات السيارات . وحول
جرائم القتل اكد ان مثل هذه الجرائم غير ملحوظة في صنعاء خلال
الفترة الاخيرة وان القتل من اجل السرقة غير موجود تقريبا . الا
انه اشار الى تَكُرار جرائم القتل الناتج عن الثأر في بعض
المحافظات الاخرى .

26 September (Yemen) 20 December 1990

HOMEWORK

1. Write one or more Arabic news stories of your own around the following groups of words and phrases:

to call a strike – to protest against – to organise a demonstration – to arrest – demonstrator – to charge (a suspect) – to deport – to be involved in – to pass sentence of ... on ... – court

political prisoner – girl – youth – to flee – to commit a crime – new facts have come to light – settler – to shoot – to claim responsibility for – to put on red alert – to acknowledge/confess

2. Write one or more Arabic news stories of your own around the following words/phrases:

toppling the regime – attempted coup – life imprisonment – to be convicted of – it is rumoured that – task – to fail – trades union – to respond to – fall in living standards

3. (a) Write an Arabic news story of your own around the following words/phrases:

gang – housebreaking – care theft – fence – suspect – (previous) record – stiffer sentencing – delinquency

(b) In Arabic, without attempting an exact translation, explain the following concepts:

(juvenile) delinquency – rehabilitation – recidivism – probation

*4. Tape

This lesson's broadcast contains two news stories. Transcribe the first story and translate it into idiomatic English. Summarise the second story in English. Make brief notes on any linguistic features that you think deserve comment.

Economic Affairs

The terminology of economic affairs used in the media is more fluid than that given in dictionaries and glossaries of management, economics, etc. In this unit, a skeleton vocabulary is used in exercises designed to develop or consolidate the following skills:

Lesson 9.2.1: oral flexibility; oral and written improvisation (explaining English concepts in Arabic when their exact equivalent is not immediately available);

Lesson 9.2.2: sustained oral translation into and out of Arabic;

Lesson 9.2.3: sustained oral translation into Arabic; oral and written improvisation; free oral translation into Arabic.

The exercises which follow each lesson contain additional vocabulary. They must be completed before moving on to the next lesson and Unit 10.

LESSON 9.1: STATE AND CONSUMER; INVESTOR AND PRODUCER

The exercises in the Classroom Practice deal with state control of the economy through taxation; the Homework exercises deal with the financial market, state and private investment, production, costs and profits.

CLASSROOM PRACTICE

9.1.1 *Oral Exercise*

Listen to the following passage, which will be read aloud twice by the teacher.

اعلنت مارغريت ثاتشر عزمها على الاستقالة من منصب رئاسة الوزراء وقد شهدت تراجعا في شعبيتها في استطلاعات الرأي خصوصا بسبب فرضها ضريبة جديدة تعرف باسم ضريبة الفَرْد او "بـول تاكس". خفّضت حكوماتها المتعاقبة ضرائب الدَّخْل وجرّدت نقابات العمال من قوتها وباعت صناعات كان يملكها القطاع العام الى القطاع الخاص. ولكن بالرغم من كل ذلك اتجه الاقتصاد نحو الركود وازدادت البطالة .

In Arabic, explain the following words/phrases:

ضريبة ـ فَرَضَ ضريبةً ـ فَرْدٌ ـ خفّض الضرائب ـ دَخْلٌ ـ نقابات العمال ـ جرّد نقابات العمال من قوتها ـ صناعة ـ القطاع العام والقطاع الخاص ـ ركود ـ بطالة

Translate the following sentences into Arabic.

1. The economy has been sliding into recession for some time.
2. The recession which Britain now faces is said to be the worst since 1935.
3. The Labour party has always accused the Conservatives of wanting to strip the unions of their power.
4. The Conservatives for their part have always accused Labour of being controlled by the unions.
5. Conservative election manifestos usually promise to lower income tax, and accuse Labour of wanting to impose new taxes.
6. The Conservatives support and are traditionally supported by the private sector.
7. The Labour party has traditionally supported the public sector.
8. Most public-sector industries in Britain have already been sold to the private sector; the government is now planning to sell off British Rail.
9. The unions have been stripped of most of their power and no longer have very much influence.

10. Unemployment is on the increase, and strikes have become a very rare occurrence.

9.1.3 Oral/Written Exercise

1. Orally, in Arabic, without attempting an exact translation, discuss and explain the meaning of the following terms:

VAT – capital gains tax – road tax – tax evasion – split-up of the public sector.

2. Explain the above terms in writing, using complete Arabic sentences.

9.1.4 Oral/Written Exercise

Listen to the following passage, which will be read aloud twice by the teacher:

قررت الحكومة الاردنية رفع ضريبة الاستهلاك بنسبة ٥٪ على بعض السِّلَع و ١٠٪ على سلع اخرى سواء المستورَدة منها او المصنوعة محليا . وقد شملت الضريبة الجديدة سلع استهلاكية مثل البسكويت والمشروبات الغازية والصابون والشامبو .

1. Orally, in Arabic, explain the following words/phrases:

رفَعَ ضريبةً ـ استهلاك ـ سِلْعَة ـ سِلَع استهلاكية ـ اِسْتوْرَدَ / اِسْتيرادٌ

2. Orally, in Arabic, discuss and explain the meaning and, where applicable, the connotations of the following terms:

the tax payer – the consumer – consumer-led – consumer durables – consumer watchdog

3. Explain the above terms in writing, using complete Arabic sentences.

9.1.5 Oral/Written Exercise

Listen to the following passage, which will be read aloud twice by the teacher:

السكر الجزائري في المغرب

ذكر رئيس الحكومة الجزائرية في حديث أجراه مع الاذاعة الجزائرية ان المغرب هو أهم مركز لتجارة السكر الجزائري الذي تساند أسعاره الدولة الجزائرية والذي يباع محليا بـ 2,50 دينار جزائري للكيلوغرام . وقال ان السكر الجزائري بسبب سعْره المنخفض يهرّب الى المغرب، وأشار الى ان مُعَدَّل استهلاك المواطن المغربي

من السكر – حسب الإحصائيات – هو 36 كلغ ، وهو رقْم مرتفع جدا .
وتحدث عن تهريب السلع المساندة أسعارها من طرف الدولة وقال
"انظروا الى حدودنا الشرقية والغربية والجنوبية والى صفوف
السيارات التي تقف في محطّات الوقود ". وقال ان مسحوق
الحليب الجزائري يباع في نيجيريا .

1. Orally, in Arabic, explain the following words/phrases:

سِعْرٌ ـ سعر منخفض ـ السِّلَع المساندَة أسْعارها من طرف الدولة ـ
تهريب السكر الجزائري الى المغرب ـ مُعَدَّل استهلاك المواطن
المغربي من السكر ـ الإحصائيات ـ رَقْم مرتفع جدا ـ وقود ـ
محطّات الوقود ـ مسحوق الحليب

al-'Alam (Rabat), 14 September 1991

2. Orally, in Arabic, without attempting an exact translation, discuss
   and explain the meanings of the following terms:

price control – incomes policy – inflation – protectionism – market forces

3. Explain the above terms in writing, using complete Arabic sentences.

HOMEWORK

1. Arabic market reports, printed or broadcast, are closely modelled on
   their English counterparts. Translate the following examples into the
   appropriate style of English:

ـ استأنفت الليرة اللبنانية تحسنها الطفيف امس في أعْقاب
استقرارها في اليومين السابقين ، وبلغ سعر صَرْف الدولار لدى
إغلاق التداول في سوق بيروت المالية 885 ليرة للشراء و886 ليرة
للبيع مقابل 885,50 ليرة للشراء و 886,50 للبيع يوم امس الاول .

ـ هبطت أسعار الأسْهُم والسَّنَدات هبوطا شديدا امس الاربعاء في
الوقت الذي ارتفعت فيه أسعار النفط الى أعلى مستوى لها منذ
نحو خمس سنوات . وقد ارتفعت أسعار النفط في أسواق نيو
يورك لتصل عند الإغلاق الى 30 دولارا للبَرْميل وهو أعلى مستوى
لأسعار النفط منذ شهر سبتمبر عام 1985 . ويتوقع المحللون
لشؤون النفط ان تصل الأسعار الى 33 دولارا للبرميل الواحد .

ـ نتائج الـ ٩ شهور الأولى في عام ١٩٩١: انخفاض طفيف في أرباح (سابيك)

حققت الشركة السعودية للصناعات الأساسية (سابيك) خلال الأشهر التسعة الاولى من هذا العام أرباحا تقدر بـ١.٩٥٢.٢٧٢ ريال مقابل ١.٩٥٩.٤٢٢ ريال في نفس الفترة من العام السابق. اعلن ذلك نائب رئيس مجلس ادارة الشركة مؤكدا ان هذه النتائج الطيبة جاءت رغم حالة عدم الاستقرار التي مر بها الاقتصاد الدولي .

2. Read the following passages, but do not translate them.

ـ دعا رئيس الوزراء اللبناني المستثمرين العرب الى تشغيل رساميلهم في لبنان والمشاركة في صندوق المساعدة العربية والدولية لإعادة تعمير البلاد .

ـ قال نور سلطان نزارباييف رئيس جمهورية كازخستان ان جمهورية كازخستان تسعى الى تعزيز علاقاتها مع الدول العربية والاسلامية. ورحب نزارباييف بالاستثمارات العربية قائلا ان بلاده تملك ذهبا ونفطا وموارد طبيعية تجعلها مكانا صالحا للاستثمار .

ـ تراجعت الاستثمارات العربية في المغرب بشكل كبير مقارنةً مع ما كانت عليه قبل حرب الخليج. واشار محللون اقتصاديون الى ان الاستثمارات السعودية وصلت عام ١٩٨٥ الى ٢٨,٥ ٪ من إجمالي الاستثمارات الاجنبية ثم انخفضت الى ٩,٨ ٪ عام ١٩٩٠ وواصلت تراجعها عام ١٩٩١. وكان توزيع مصادر الاستثمار في المغرب خلال السنه الماضية على الشكل التالي : ٤٧,٦ ٪ للدول الاوروبية و ٢٥,٧ ٪ للدول العربية .

Use the vocabulary that they contain to write one or more Arabic news stories of your own around the following words/phrases:

investment – investor – source of investment – a good place to invest – natural resources – reconstruction – distribution – employment – total – economic analyst

3. Read the following passages, but do not translate them.

ـ يُنْفِق المستهلك المصري نصف دخله على الطعام والشراب،
وينفق حوالى ٢٠٪ منه على الخدمات . أما الباقي فيوزع بين
المَلْبَس والمَسْكَن والوقود .

ـ ان الاحتلال الاسرائيلي للأراضي الفلسطينية احتلال مُرْبِح لأن
الأراضي المحتلة تشكل سوقا للصادرات الاسرائيلية وخاصة للسلع
الاستهلاكية ولأن هذه السوق قريبة من مواقع الإنتاج مما يساعد
على خفض تَكْلِفَة النقل التي تعتبر عاملا مهما في العلاقات
التجارية بين الدول .

ـ لم تكشف الحكومة الاسرائيلية بعد عن التكلفة الإجمالية
لمشروعها الاستيطاني الجديد، غير انه من المتوقع ان يكلّف
مليارات الدولارات .

Use the vocabulary that they contain to write one of more Arabic news
stories of your own around the following words/phrases:

to spend – food, drink, clothes, housing, fuel and services – profitable –
transport costs – total costs

4. Read the following passages, but do not translate them.

ـ بذلت الحكومة المصرية جهودا كبيرة لزيادة الإنتاج ورفع نسبة
الصادرات وخفض الواردات . وبالرغم من ذلك فإن نسبة
الاستهلاك تتزايد ويتوقع ان يبلغ حجم الاستهلاك النهائي ٥٠
مليار جنيه مصري في نهاية السنة . وقد بلغ معدل نمو الاستهلاك
العائلي نحو ٥٪ بما يمثل ٩٪ من جملة الاستهلاك النهائي .

ـ تباينت ردود الفعل المغربية حول التخفيض الذي لَحِقَ الدرهم
المغربي الاسبوع الماضي والذي بلغ ٩,٥٪ في مقابل معظم العُمْلات
الاوروبية . واعتبر رجال اعمال وشركات عاملة في مجال التصدير
هذا الإجراء مبادرة تساعد على زيادة حجم الصادرات ودعم قدرتها
التنافسية داخل الاسواق الدولية . واشارت مصادر اقتصادية في
الرباط الى ان صندوق النقد الدولي ظل يطالب بخفض قيمة
العُمْلة المغربية التي يعتقد انها أغْلى من قيمتها الحقيقية .

ـ قالت وكالة الانباء العمانية ان وزير الطاقة العماني سعيد بن أحمد الشنفري سيناقش تعزيز علاقات التعاون بين منظمة البلدان المصدّرة للبترول "اوبك" والدول المُنْتِجة للنفط غير الأعضاء في المنظمة خلال زيارته لاندونيسيا . وقَد قامت عمان ـ وهي من الدول المنتجة غير الأعضاء في "اوبك" ـ بدور رئيسي في جمع الدول الأعضاء في "اوبك" والمنتجين المستقلين لمناقشة الإجراءات الواجب القيام بها لتحقيق استقرار أسعار النفط . وقالت الوكالة ان وزير الطاقة سافر امس الى استراليا لإجراء مناقشات مع مسؤولين بشأن استخدام التكنولوجيا الحديثة في إنتاج النفط والغاز .

Use the vocabulary that they contain to write one or more Arabic news stories of your own around the following words/phrases:

currency – value – devaluation – competitiveness – OPEC – non-OPEC – energy – price stability – imports and exports – volume (of trade, etc.)

*5. Tape

This lesson's broadcast contains three stories. Transcribe the first story and translate it into idiomatic English. Summarise the second and third stories in English. Make brief notes on any linguistic features that you think deserve comment.

LESSON 9.2: DEVELOPING ECONOMIES: FINANCE, MATERIALS AND SUPPLY

The exercises in the Classroom Practice deal with Third World dependency on foreign investment and aid and consolidate the vocabulary learnt in Lesson 9.1; the Homework exercises introduce vocabulary relating to materials and supply and costs, with particular reference to loans and debts, mainly in the context of developing economies.

CLASSROOM PRACTICE

9.2.1 Oral Exercise

Translate the following passage, section by section, into Arabic:

The devaluation of the Moroccan dirham was expected to lead to an increase in foreign investment, / and its announcement was greeted with relief by Moroccan businessmen. / The Moroccan currency was felt to be overvalued against most European currencies; / with devaluation, the Moroccan government expected European governments and businessmen to invest more in the country's developing industries. / The idea was to boost the volume of local production and exports, / and to scale down the country's reliance on costly imports. / But devaluation is a risky business, and often fails because of unexpected factors. / The unexpected factor here was the Gulf War. / France and Germany had been Morocco's main European trading partners, / but, because of their role in financing the Gulf War, they now have less money to invest abroad than in the 1980s. / Morocco used to rely heavily on tourism, and was very popular with wealthy German tourists; / but in the wake of the Gulf conflict, western tourists have been reluctant to visit Muslim countries, including Morocco. / Morocco, as a developing country, relies heavily on foreign subsidies. / The IMF has promised Morocco an economic and social package designed to develop local industries, particularly private-sector industries. / But such development also depends on increased Arab investment, and Arab investment in North Africa has fallen off. / It looks as if foreign investors may continue to show reluctance to invest in Moroccan businesses if the world economic situation fails to improve. / The fact is that both Europe and the USA are facing a long period of recession. / The failure of international trade negotiations shows that the European Community for its part is prepared to defend its own agricultural and manufacturing industries against competition from the Third World and developing countries. / It is perhaps odd that the IMF and the World Bank, which represent the industrially-developed western nations, should have the power to impose packages entailing radical change on countries like Morocco, / while at the same time the West does not hesitate to take steps that will inevitably lead to the failure of such packages and the policies they impose / if western economic interests demand it, regardless of the effect this may have on the world economy in the long run.

9.2.2 *Oral Exercise*

Translate the following passage, in relatively informal Arabic, orally into idiomatic English, section by section. Guess the meaning of any unfamiliar terms. Repeat the exercise, if necessary, until fluency is achieved.

في جولة تفقّدية لمشروعات صناعية وزراعية جديدة أقيمت بمدينة السادات / قال الرئيس حسني مبارك ان على المواطن المصري ان يستخدم أمواله للتنمية في بلاده ./ وأضاف الرئيس ان المواطن أغنى من الحكومة / وان من المستحيل ان تقوم الحكومة بكل شيء ./ وقال ان مستقبلنا في زيادة العمل والإنتاج خلال الفترة القادمة / خاصة ونحن نرى التحولات التي تجري في العالم./ قال الرئيس مبارك : علينا ان ننتج ونشتغل / ونقلل من الكلام ونكثر من العمل / وإلا فإننا سنعاني خلال السنوات السبع او الثماني القادمة / لأن العالم كله يطور نفسه في التكنولوجيا بما في ذلك الدول الشرقية ./ ويكون السؤال هو : الى من سنصدر ومع من نتعامل؟ / إذن لا بد ان ننتج / ونبحث عن أسواق لنا في الخارج / سواء أسواق عربية او افريقية او في دول اخرى ./ وإن لم نسبق فسوف نتأخر ويفوتنا القطار ./ لا بد ان نطور أنفسنا بما يتمشى مع الظروف المستقبلية / وننتج ونشجع القطاع الخاص بقدر ما نستطيع / ونعمل على تطوير القطاع العام ./

وعقب جولته بمدينة السادات قام الرئيس بجولة اخرى / تفقد خلالها مشروعات القطاع الخاص الزراعية / على طريق مصر - الاسكندرية الصحراوي ./ وشاهد الرئيس خلال ثلاث ساعات اخرى قاد فيها سيارته بنفسه / المزارع التي حولت الطريق من اللون الأصفر الى الأخضر ./ وفي حديثه خلال عودته الى القاهرة اعرب الرئيس مبارك عن سعادته لمشروعات القطاع الخاص في الصناعة والزراعة ./ وقال : " لقد زرت مدينة السادات في مرة سابقة / وشاهدت فيها عدة مصانع صغيرة تعد على أصابع اليد الواحدة ./ ولاحظت اليوم ان المصانع كبيرة وكلها للقطاع الخاص "./ وقال : من المستحيل ان تقوم الحكومة بكل شيء ./ ولقد رأينا أمامنا مثيلا

واضحا للدول التي كانت تريد القيام بكل شيء / ولو لم ترد ان تقوم بكل شيء / ما كان قد حدث ما حدث في الفترة الماضية في الدول الشرقية ./ وقال الرئيس : لا بد ان نشجع القطاع الخاص / مصريا كان او عربيا او اجنبيا / وانني أعطي الأُوْلَوِيّة للمصري والعربي./ فليحضر الى مدينة السادات ويقيم مصانع / او يقيم ما شاء من مشروعات./ وأضاف الرئيس : هناك في مصر مدن كثيرة جديدة / وبها تسهيلات / ونشجع أية مشروعات ./ وقال : اذا كنا الآن نأخذ المَعُونة من بعض الدول ، فمع التغييرات الموجودة في العالم اليوم سيأتي وقت وتقل فيه المعونة بالتدريج ./ فلا بد ان نطور أنفسنا بحيث لا نأخذ معونة من احد ./ ومن معه أموال لا بد ان يستخدمها ./ نشجع القطاع الخاص بقدر ما نستطيع ./ أما القطاع العام فنحن نعمل على تطويره ./ لكن ما حدث الآن هو ان شركة خاسرة ندفع لها أرباحا ./ وعندنا شركات مشتركة تدخل الحكومة فيها بجزء والقطاع الخاص بجزء / ولا بد ان نجدها خاسرة ./ وهذه كلها مشروعات تعود الى اعوام ١٩٧٨، ١٩٧٩ /ونعاني منها الآن ونحاول إصلاحها./ أمامنا مشاكل كثيرة / ولا نيأس ، وعلينا ان نعمل بدلا من ان نقول / "هذه شركة مشتركة لا بد ان نبيعها". / علينا ان نرفع مستواها وندع القطاع الخاص يأخذها ويديرها ./

وقال الرئيس : كيف سنعيش ؟ / عدد السكان في مصر يزيد اكثر من مليون نَسَمَة كل عام ، فكيف سنعيش ؟ / انني لست يساريا ولا يمينيا / ولكنني كمواطن مصري أنظر من وجهة النظر العملية ماذا نفعل ./ علينا أن ندع النظريات جانبا ./ لقد شاهدت نظريات فشلت واخرى ستفشل في المستقبل ./ والله لست يساريا ولا يمينيا وانني ادع النظريات جانبا ./ انني آخذ ما يلائمني من هنا وما يتناسب معي من هناك / وأسير في طريقي ./ تفكيري ليس نظرية قرأتها / ولا شيئا من هذا القبيل./انني مواطن عادي/ أفكر هل هذا ينفعنا في ظروفنا هذه ؟ / آخذ من هنا وهناك ما يلائمني / واذا وجدت عائدا جيدا وإنتاجا جيدا / فأهلا وسهلا ./ واذا لم أجده جيدا أغيره ./ يجب ان نكون واقعيين ومَنْطِقيين / وان نعيش في الواقع ونشتغل ونبذل مجهودا / ومن معه فلوس يتفضل ويشتري أرضا / ونسهل له الحصول عليها .

al-Ahrām, 27 December 1989

HOMEWORK

1. Use the following words/phrases in an Arabic news story of your own:

تَأَخَّرَ ـ فات + ﻩ ـ القطار ـ مَصْنَعٌ ـ أُوْلَوِيّة ـ تَسهيلات ـ مَعُونَةٌ ـ نَسَمَةٌ ـ عائدٌ ـ واقعيّ ـ مَنْطِقيّ

2. Comment briefly on the word formations and usages underlined below, and give their idiomatic English equivalents.

ـ **ضربت** البطالة قطاعات واسعة من القوى العاملة خلال الأعوام الثلاثة الماضية .

ـ تقوم الحكومة الاسرائيلية بتنفيذ خطّة استيطانية **واسعة النِّطاق** في النقب . ستضم المنطقة الاستيطانية المقترحة مدن استيطانية ومؤسسات تكنولوجية ومؤسسات أبحاث في شؤون **استزراع** الأراضي بعد **استصلاحها**. وقد دعا دفيد بن جوريون أول رئيس وزراء اسرائيل منذ أوائل الخمسينات الى تطوير النقب استيطانيا وزراعيا لـ **استيعاب** ملايين اليهود فيه .

ـ تنفيذا للتوجيهات السامية لحضرة صاحب الجلالة السلطان قابوس بن سعيد المعظم ـ حفظه الله ـ وجهود حكومة جلالته الرشيدة الرامية الى **تنشيط الحركة الاقتصادية** في البلاد، أعلن معالي أحمد بن سويدان البلوشي وزير البريد **والبرق** والهاتف ورئيس الهيئة العامة لـ **لمواصلات السلكية واللاسلكية** عن تخفيض أسعار المكالمات الهاتفية .

ـ فلقو تبدأ حملة تسويق مكثّفة في منطقة الخليج

3. Read the following passages, but do not translate them.

ـ اعلن في أنقرة ان تركيا ستزوّد ايران بالكهرباء ابتداء من العام المقبل ولمدة عشرة اعوام . وطبقا لاتفاقية أُبرمت بهذا الصدد بين هيئة الكهرباء التركية والاتحاد الايراني للكهرباء فإن المعدل السنوي لتزويد ايران بالكهرباء سيكون حوالى مائة مليون كيلووات ساعة قابلة للزيادة بنسبة ٢٥ بالمائة اذا طلبت ايران ذلك.

ـ بدأت جمهوريات آسيا الوسطى تشكيل اتحاد جديد والتنسيق بين سياساتها الاقتصادية. تتركز بهذه الجمهوريات زراعة القطن والأرز وتربية الاغنام ويوجد بها كذلك النفط والغاز الطبيعي والمعادن الاخرى . تحت الحكم السوفياتي كانت هذه الجمهوريات تمدّ روسيا بالموادّ الخام † والموادّ الغذائية، إلا انها الآن تملك فرصة لتنمية مواردها بشكل أفضل حيث وضعت برامج خاصة بتحفيز الاستثمار وجذب المستثمرين الاجانب .

ـ قال الرئيس مبارك : الحكومة توفّر الأمن والاستقرار للمواطن حتى يستخدم أمواله للتنمية في بلاده . فإن هذه الأموال تساهم في تشغيل العمالة وتوفّر لنا أموالا تغنينا عن المعونات التي نأخذها حاليا من بعض الدول .

Use the vocabulary that they contain to write an Arabic news story of your own around the following words/phrases:

to supply – to provide – minerals – raw materials – foodstuffs – to attract – to give incentives to – to develop resources – sheep-farming – cotton-farming

4. Read the following passages, but do not translate them.

ـ بدأ امس تطبيق الزيادة الجديدة في أسعار تذاكر الطائرات الصادرة من القاهرة . وتطبق هذه الزيادة على جميع شركات الطيران بهدف إحداث توازن بين سعر صَرْف الجنيه المصري وغيره من العملات الاجنبية . وقد تم الاتفاق في هذا الصدد مع منظمة "الياتا" التي تضم شركات الطيران العالمية لمواجهة ارتفاع سعر تشغيل الطائرات .

ـ تقرر ان ترفع الصحف المغربية سعر بيعها من درهم واحد الى درهم ونصف درهم. وسيدخل القرار حَيِّزَ التنفيذ ابتداء من أول فبراير المقبل .

ـ قررت الحكومة خفض سعر الفائدة وذلك لتنشيط الحركة الاقتصادية في البلاد .

†Note that *khām* is invariable in this phrase.

Use the words and phrases underlined to write an Arabic news story of your own around the following English words/phrases:

to come into effect – interest rate – rate of exchange – running costs – retail price

5. Read the following passages, but do not translate them.

- في خطاب ألقاه امس في افتتاح المؤتمر الثالث عشر لاتحاد البرلمانات الافريقية دعا الرئيس حسني مبارك الجماعة الدولية الى بذل جهودها من اجل التوصل الى حل لمشكلة المَدْيُونِيَّة الافريقية التي بلغت ٤٤٠ مليار دولار .

- مصادر مغربية : خفض سعر الدرهم مرتبط بمفاوضات إعادة جَدْوَلَة الديون
لم تستبعد مصادر مالية مغربية ان تكون لعملية خفض العملة المغربية علاقة بـ جَدْوَلَة ٣٫٢ مليون دولار من دُيون المغرب .

- اعلنت المانيا انها سَتُعفي بلندا من نصف الديون المستحقة عليها والبالغة ٥ مليار دولار وذلك لمساندة الاصلاحات الاقتصادية التي تطبقها وارسو. وستسمح الحكومة الالمانية لبلندا بـ سَداد النصف الباقي من الدَّيْن خلال ١٨ عاما .

- على ان يتم سدادها بالجنيه : قروض بـ الدولار للمستثمرين المصريين
قررت الحكومة المصرية السماح للمستثمرين المصريين بالحصول على قروض بالدولار لإقامة مشروعات صغيرة على ان يتم السداد بالجنيه المصري وبعد فترة سماح ٣ سنوات او اكثر. وستختلف فَتَرات السماح حسب طبيعة المشروع وقد تصل فترة السماح لأكثر من خمس سنوات. وسيتم سداد القَرْض بـ فائدة ميسَّرة تبلغ ٥٪ سنويا وتصل بذلك الى نصف أسعار الفائدة الحالية على القروض المماثلة .

ـ اخذت الحكومة الاردنية اجراءات لتخفيف **العَجْز في ميزانية** الدولة وقررت رفع ضريبة استهلاكية بنسبة ٥٪ على بعض السلع.

ـ **عَجْز قياسي في الموازنة** الامريكية

ارتفع العجز في الموازنة الامريكية خلال **السنة المالية** الحالية ليصل الى رقم قياسي. والرقم القياسي السابق سُجّل في عام ١٩٨٦. و **قيمة العَجْز** الحالي ٢٦٨ مليار دولار مقابل ٢٢ مليار دولار في **العام المالي** السابق.

Use the words and phrases underlined to write one or more Arabic news stories of your own around the following English words/phrases:

debt – (in)debt(edness) – to reschedule a debt – to write off a debt – outstanding debt – to repay a debt – to borrow in dollars and repay in pounds – small businesses – record figure – period of repayment – easy terms/preferential rate of interest (on) – financial year – balance of payments – budget deficit – the amount of the deficit

*6. Tape

This lesson's broadcast contains three news stories. Transcribe the first story and translate it into idiomatic English. Summarise the second and third stories in English. Make brief notes on any linguistic features that you think deserve comment.

LESSON 9.3: ECONOMIC PRESSURES AND ECONOMIC MIGRATION

Half the exercises in the Classroom Practice apply the vocabulary of Lessons 9.1 and 9.2, and some new vocabulary relating to population growth, to the topic of the economic pressures experienced by states and individuals; other exercises introduce new English economic terms for improvised translation. Further vocabulary relating to population changes and the economic pressures or natural disasters which cause them is covered in the Homework exercises.

CLASSROOM PRACTICE

9.3.1 Oral Exercise

Translate the following passage orally into Arabic, section by section.

In spite of the facilities which the government has made available to small businesses, / the number of loss-making businesses, be they small or large, has reached record figures. / The ordinary investor is looking for a good return on his money; / not surprisingly, it is the big companies which can be expected to make a steady profit that have attracted the most investment. / Until recently, these companies were indeed making record profits; but that was before the recession. / Now, many former profit-making concerns have turned into loss-makers, / and economic analysts tell us that this trend is on the increase. / There have been calls for a cut in interest rates to stimulate the economy, and for more government schemes giving incentives to investors; / meanwhile, profits and share prices are falling sharply all the time. / The average income is also falling, along with living standards, because of unemployment, / and the average family's living costs are rising; / for though the prices of some consumer goods have been slashed, the cost of everything else – from food to electricity and telephone calls – continues to rise.

9.3.2 Oral/ Written Exercise

1. Read the following passages. Orally, in Arabic, without attempting an exact translation, discuss and explain the words and phrases in italics.

   A company spokesman, responding to a *survey* of air passengers in which the company was *ranked* twentieth out of fifty carriers, said that *passengers vote with their feet*, and that his company was still the world's largest carrier.

   A scheme set up by a major clothes manufacturer aims to *bridge the gap between young designers and the marketplace*. Under the scheme, prize-winning designs will be *promoted* in selected stores under the company's own label.

2. In Arabic, in writing, convey the basic meaning of the above passages.

9.3.3 Reading Exercise

Silently read the following passage and quickly assimilate the words and phrases underlined.

كتب محلل اقتصادي عربي في مجلة "الاقتصادي" البريطانية :
يقف الوطن العربي على أبواب التسعينات وهو يواجه احتمالات
كبيرة و تحدِّيات كبيرة .فـ التحول الديموغرافي يمثل اكبر
التحديات إذ تتوقع زيادة السكان العرب من حوالي ١١٠ ملايين
نسمة عام ١٩٧٠ الى ما يزيد عن ٢٤٠ مليون نسمة عام ٢٠٠٠. أما
الأسواق المالية العربية فالمتوقع انها ستتوسع وإن اختلفت أسباب
التوسع بين قطر عربي وآخر. أما في البلاد النفطية فيتوقع
حدوث التوسع بسبب التحسين المنتظر في أسعار النفط. أما في
البلاد غير النفطية فهناك احتمال تزايد استثمارات البلاد
النفطية .

9.3.4 Oral Exercise

Translate the following passage orally into Arabic, section by section. Try to keep up an even speed with as few hesitations as possible.

In an interview with the *Financial Times*, an economic expert has predicted the the big demographic changes that are taking place in the Arab world will affect both the labour and the money markets in the region. / He said that a predicted population increase of some 100,000,000 was the biggest challenge facing the Arab economies. / The population is rising fastest in Egypt, and in North Africa, where industry is weakest and employment opportunities fewest, / and this is affecting population distribution not only in the rest of the Arab world, but also in Europe, as young North Africans leave home to seek work in the EC. / Oil prices, meanwhile, are falling worldwide, and it is uncertain whether the Arab oil-producing countries will maintain their current level of investment in the non-oil-producing countries / and thereby help to solve the latter's mounting economic and social problems, by helping to reconstruct their industrial base. / The oil-rich Arab countries prefer to invest in Japan, the EC and the USA, but inter-Arab investment has scored some successes in the past, / the new desert cities in Egypt being an oft-cited example, though there are other, less publicised examples; / and some North African countries, particularly Morocco, have been successful in attracting Common Market investment and in developing their trade with Europe. / But the burden of debt continues to grow in the non-oil-producing countries, along with the population, / and aid and investment alone will not solve their problems, which are wide-ranging and demand reconstruction on almost every level. / In addition, these countries face growing competition from other developing countries in their search for foreign markets, / while very soon, a united western Europe will probably agree on a common programme of investment and economic development for eastern Europe, / which could add to the competition already faced by developing industries elsewhere.including the Middle East. / There is also the growing fear that the EC may repatriate large numbers of young North Africans who are driven to seek work there by unemployment at home, / and whom it will be difficult to absorb into the local workforce, thus increasing the factors leading to instability in the region. / However, the developing eastern European economies will certainly need oil, much of which will be supplied by Arab producers, and this could benefit the non-oil-producing Arab countries indirectly if the profits are reinvested in the Arab world. / But if oil prices remain low, Arab investors may continue to look elsewhere for quicker profits than those afforded by inter-Arab investments. / Perhaps the major disincentive to investment in the region is the continuing threat of political instability, represented by the growing popularity of Islamic movement; / but this in its turn should encourage the more conservative Arab states, and the EC, to play a much more active role in financing development.

9.3.5 Oral/Written Exercise

1. Read the following passages. Orally, in Arabic, without attempting an exact translation, discuss and explain the words and phrases underlined.

   An *enterprise company* is to be *launched* shortly in South Wales to help local companies market their products more *effectively*. It will offer a *cost-sharing arrangement* ranging from *market research* to publicity, appointing distributors and setting up *joint exhibitions*.

   It was revealed yesterday that there was a jump of £300m in manufac-turers' stocks of *finished goods*, suggesting that *demand has faded faster than industry's ability to adapt*. Analysts pointed out that *involuntary stock-building* is an *early symptom* of recession.

2. In Arabic, in writing, convey the basic meaning of the above passages.

9.3.6 Oral Exercise

Listen to the following passage, which will be read aloud once by the teacher. It will then be read aloud, section by section, for you to translate orally into Arabic.

1. Adopt whatever style you think appropriate; paraphrase, abridge or pad where necessary to achieve a fluent translation.
2. Analyse and discuss any points of difficulty.

X: We're in the middle of Britain's worst recession for fifty years, and small businesses are folding right and left. What do you do when your business goes bust? *Consumer Concern* interviewed two couples from different parts of the country to find out how they were coping. First, Jonquil and Tim from Cumbria in the north. – Jonquil, Tim, what was your line of business, and why did it fail? /

J: We were sheep-farmers,and, as you know, farming has been going through a bad patch, with the changes in EC law and agricultural policy that have come into effect recently,and the recession and so on. /

T: We weren't getting anything like a good enough return on farming, so we tried to diversify. /

X: Diversification is the name of the game in farming these days, isn't it? So you branched out; how? /

J: I started doing bed-and-breakfasts; Tim started a market garden. But it was hard work, and we had to borrow heavily from the bank just to keep going, with custom falling off through the recession. The debts just kept piling up; we couldn't meet the repayments. Finally, we went under. /

X: So, Tim, Jonquil, what does the future hold for you now? /

T: Not a lot. We've lost the farm. I can't get another job. Too much unemployment in the area, for one thing. I'm too old, for another. /

X: A sad story. – Our second couple are Anne and Marmaduke, from Kent in the south-east, the region which has been worst hit by white-collar unemployment. – Marmaduke, tell us what happened to you and Anne. /

M: I didn't have my own business, like Tim and Jonquil. I was assistant editor on the local paper. Our running costs had been rising for years; all our costs started to spiral. We couldn't afford the new technology to attract more readers and compete with the tabloids; the more readers we lost, the less we could afford to improve the paper. It was a vicious circle. The paper closed down a year ago, and I've been without work since. /

A: Unemployment is running very high locally. There's nothing for people like Marmaduke, except for voluntary work. I've gone back to teaching, part-time, but you know what teachers' pay is like. /

X: Another very sad story, which could be replicated up and down the country.

HOMEWORK

1. Read the following passages, but do not translate them.

ـ طلبت دول خليجية من الأمم المتحدة مساعدة فَنّية ومالية لإصلاح الأضرار الناتجة عن احتراق آبار النفط في الكويت خلال حرب الخليج .

ـ قال مسؤول خليجي ان دول منطقة الخليج تحتاج الى تمويل عاجل للقضاء على تلوث البيئة الناتج عن احتراق آبار النفط الكويتية خلال حرب الخليج . وأوضح المسؤول ان تقديرات التكاليف تزيد عن ١٠.٢ بليون دولار .

يمر القطاع الصناعي اللبناني بأسوأ حالاته نتيجة الهَدْم والدَّمار الذين عصفا بلبنان مؤخرا . وتقول مصادر لبنانية ان خسائر الأحداث الأخيرة تقدر قيمتها بأربعمائة مليون دولار تضاف الى ذلك الخسائر الناتجة عن قطع التيّار الكهربائي . وقال متحدث باسم جمعية الصناعيين اللبنانيين ان الجمعية ستطلب تعويضا عن الأضرار التي لحقت بالمصانع .

ـ يتوقع ان يصل عدد المهاجرين اليهود من روسيا الى فلسطين المحتلة الى ٤٠٠ الف مهاجر خلال هذا العام . وكان عدد سكان اسرائيل شهد تزايدا كبيرا خلال العام الماضي بسبب تدفق المهاجرين السوفيات الى البلاد . وذكرت إحصائية اسرائيلية رسمية ان نسبة الزيادة السكانية بلغت ٨ ٪ خلال سنة ١٩٩١ مقابل ٦,٢ ٪ في السنة ١٩٩٠ و ١,٦ ٪ في العام السابق . وأشارت الإحصائية الى ان عدد السكان وصل الآن الى اكثر من ٥ مليون نسمة بينهم ٩٠٠ الف فلسطيني يشكلون ١٨ ٪ من مجموع السكان.

Use the vocabulary that they contain to write one or more Arabic news stories of your own around the following words/phrases:

damage – loss – destruction – estimated cost – estimated losses of ... – caused by/resulting from – repair – compensation – emigrant – to pour into (e.g. emigrants into a country) – population – population increase – total population

2. Read the following passages, but do not translate them.

ـ تلقت اثيوبيا وعودا بمساعدات قيمتها ٦٠٠ مليون دولار في شكل معونات لتنفيذ برنامج طارئ لإعادة البناء والإصلاح . واعلن ان البنك الدولي والمجموعة الاقتصادية الاوروبية وبنك التنمية الافريقي ومنظمات دولية اخرى ستقدم الأموال في شكل منح وقروض . وتستخدم المساعدات في بناء مدارس وإعادة بناء القطاعين الصناعي والزراعي في اثيوبيا .

ـ اكد السيد بيتر اوراث المندوب السامي لشؤون اللاجئين بالسودان ان اكثر من ثلاثمائة وخمسين الف لاجئ يحتاجون الى مساعدات عاجلة لمواجهة سوء التغذية وتوفير أسباب الحياة الكريمة لهؤلاء اللاجئين . وقال اوراث ان الحكومة السودانية تبذل جهودا كبيرا لحل مشكلة اللاجئين الذين يتزايد عددهم باستمرار .

ـ زلزال جديد في ايران

فر العديد من سكان مدينة بهبهان الواقعة في جنوب ايران والتي تعرضت لعشرات من الهزّات الأرضية من منازلهم ويعيشون في الخيام . وأوضح متحدث باسم الحكومة الايرانية ان آخر زلزال تعرضت له المدينة الليلة قبل الماضية بلغت قوته خمس درجات بمقْياس ريختر .

ـ تفيد الأنباء ان عدد الجَوْعى والمتشردين في ازدياد في المدن الامريكية . وجاء في التقارير ان الطلبات للحصول على معونات غِذائية ازدادت هذا العام بنسبة ٢٥ في المائة .

ـ فَيَضانات بالمغرب وهزّة أرضية في تايوان

سببت فيضانات اجتاحت منطقة الفنيدق بإقليم تطوان شمال المغرب إلحاق أضرار بمائة سيارة وإتلاف السلع في ستين محلاً تجاريا .

من جهة اخرى ضربت هزة أرضية بلغت قوتها ٢ . ٦ درجات بمقياس ريختر جنوب مدينة هوالين على الساحل الشرقي لتايوان امس . ولم يعلن عن حدوث أضرار او خسائر .

ـ اعلنت منطقة الخليج منطقة متضررة بعد احتراق أبار النفط الكويتية خلال حرب الخليج .

ـ اعلنت منظمات الأمم المتحدة والمنظمات الإنسانية الطّوْعية الأخرى العاملة في مجال الإغاثة عن تقديرها لعمليات إعادة تسكين اللاجئين الاثيوبيين ووعدت بتقديم الدعم اللازم لهذه العمليات .

Use the vocabulary that they contain to write one or more Arabic news stories of your own around the following words/phrases:

urgent – emergency (adjective) – humanitarian – voluntary – homeless – hungry – grants and loans – aid valued at … – technical aid – food aid – malnutrition – tent – rehousing – refugee – UN High Commissioner for Refugees – flood – earthquake – earth tremor – disaster area

*3. Tape
This lesson's broadcast contains two news stories. Transcribe the first story and translate it into idiomatic English. Summarise the second story in English. Make brief notes on any linguistic features that you think deserve comment.

Disaster and Aid

GENERAL REMARKS

This unit consists of exercises designed to consolidate skills of oral translation into Arabic and aural comprehension.

From the linguistic point of view, it should be noted that disaster reports carried by the Arabic press are often direct translations of English-language reports supplied by international news agencies.

LESSON 10.1: DISASTER REPORTS

CLASSROOM PRACTICE

10.1.1 Oral Exercise

Listen to the following passage, which will be read aloud, section by section, by the teacher. Translate it orally into Arabic. Try to keep up an even speed with as few hesitations as possible. Repeat the exercise, if necessary, until fluency is achieved.

As floods again swept the south of the country yesterday, casualties mounted and thousands of people fled their homes. / Flooding in other parts of the country has already caused severe damage to homes and vehicles; / losses to industry have been heavy, and are estimated at several billion dollars. / Leading manufacturers have complained of power cuts and say that they will be asking the government for compensation for lost production. / The west of the country has been declared a disaster area, after an earthquake last week which registered 5.6 on the Richter scale / Thousands of people are living in tents, and the number of homeless is increasing daily. / Voluntary agencies have mounted emergency operations to aid the hungry and homeless, / and several foreign governments are expected to offer humanitarian aid within the next few days. / The UN High Commissioner for Refugees has already announced that aid worth over a billion dollars is to be sent to the country to help it deal with its refugee problem. /

Tens of thousands of refugees from neighbouring countries poured across the northern border into camps last autumn, / most of them suffering from malnutrition as a result of the ten-year-old civil war which has brought agriculture in the region to a virtual standstill. / The government has received medical and food aid from a number of UN relief organisations, / and technical aid from other international agencies to help with rehousing the refugees; / all this at a time when the country's economy is already under severe strain following a sharp increase in the population / due to the return home of hundreds of thousands of emigrants in the wake of the Gulf War. / These people now form five per cent of the total population, / and the government faces the task of rehousing them and absorbing them into the workforce at a time of mounting unemployment, / when the country has been hit by a sharp drop in its production of oil, the mainstay of the economy, / following the burning of many of its oil wells, which sustained heavy shelling during the civil war./ – News just in from the disaster area says that twelve people died when a bulldozer engaged in rescue work overturned, / and that hundreds more were buried alive when their homes collapsed on them in the latest of a series of earth tremors, bringing the death toll in the region to over 2,000.

10.1.2 Aural/Written Exercise

1. Listen to the five following passages, which will be read aloud by the teacher. The first three will each be read twice, and the last two will each be read three times. For each passage, in writing, identify the type of disaster or violence and number of victims or type of aid and its value, making notes of any new vocabulary in the relevant area. Ignore any other information.

2. Compare your notes with the texts below, and discuss any points of difficulty.

١ـ اعلن ناطق باسم وزارة الخارجية الصينية ان انهيارات أرضية كبيرة وقعت امس أسفرت عن مقتل ٢١٦ شخصا في مقاطعة يونان الجنوبية . وقال ان ستين عائلة دفنت خلال دقيقتين وقتل ٥١٧ شخصا على الفور في حين أصيب سبعة آخرين بجروح .

٢ـ بدأ امس برنامج طارئ للأمم المتحدة لمساعدة مواطني انجولا في المناطق التي تعاني من المجاعة . ونقل راديو صوت أمريكا عن المسؤولين في الأمم المتحدة ان اول قافلة للأغذية غادرت ميناء† لوبيتو الانجولي امس متوجهة الى بلدة هوامير الانجولية .

٣ـ قتل نحو ثلاث آلاف جندي من جيش تحرير شعب السودان خلال اشتباكات طائفية بين أنصار جون قرنق وأنصار لام اكول أمس . وتفيد الأنباء الواردة من الخرطوم ان المعْركة التي استمرت خمسة أيام وقعت في ولاية معالي النيل . وقال عمال الإغاثة في نيروبي ان بعض المتمردين فرواالى كينيا واثيوبيا بعد ان فقدوا أسلحتهم في المعركة او باعوها ليشتروا بها طعاما . ويذكر ان الخلاف قد نشب بين جون قرنق ولام اكول بسبب إصرار قرنق على القتال من اجل إقامة دولة سودانية علمانية ومتحدة بينما يرغب اكول في انفصال الجنوب .

٤ـ ذكر مسؤولون في الخارجية الامريكية ان ادارة جورج بوش تعتزم إجراء خفض في مساعداتها العسكرية الخارجية لعام ١٩٩٢ باستثناء اثنين من المستفيدين التقليديين هما اسرائيل ومصر . وقال خبير في الخارجية الامريكية ان الخفض سيكون بمعدل ٣٠ في المائة اذا تم سحب هذين البلدين من برنامج المساعدات لكنه سيكون بمعدل ١١ ٪ مع بقائهما داخل البرنامج .

†The word *mīnā'*, given as feminine in the dictionaries, is generally treated as masculine in the media.

٥ـ تجتاح منطقة الشرق الاوسط منذ اسبوع موجة من الأمطار والثلوج فاقت معدلات هطولها ما هو متوقع لهذه الفترة من الشتاء . إلا ان الخبراء يؤكدون ان المنطقة تتجه نحو الجَفاف ، وقال خبير ان منطقة الشرق الاوسط ستواجه في حدود العام ١٩٩٥ أزمة مياه خطيرة تموت خلالها الزراعات بسبب الجفاف .

10.1.3 *Aural/Written Exercise*

1. Listen to the following miscellany of news stories dealing with disasters, aid and other topics, which will be read aloud once by the teacher. Each story in it will then be read aloud twice. Summarise each story in English, and make notes on any new vocabulary.

2. Compare your summaries and notes with the texts below, and discuss any points of difficulty.

١ـ صرح حاكم إقليم تارلاك بالفلبين امس بأن نحو ٤٤ الف فلبيني تم إجلاؤهم الى مخيمات في اعقات ثورة بُركان تهددهم بالمجاعة . وذكر في مقابلة اذاعية ان الفيضانات والانهيارات الطينية والجسور المنهارة تعوق وصول الشاحنات التي تحمل المعونة الغذائية الى المنطقة . ومع ذلك اكد ان شاحنتين تحملان مواد إغاثة وصلت الى المنطقة المنكوبة اليوم .

٢ـ ذكر مصدر عسكري اسرائيلي ان سلطات الاحتلال الصهيوني قد أبقت امس لليوم العاشر على التوالي حَظْر التجوّل المفروض على رام الله في الضفة الغربية بعد مقتل مستوطنين اسرائيليين. ورفع حظر التجول لمدة ثلاث ساعات امس ليتمكن السكان من التزويد بالمواد الغذائية. وشمل حظر التجول حوالى ٧٠ الف فلسطيني اضطروا الى البقاء في منازلهم منذ ديسمبر (كانون الاول) الماضي. وقد شكا السكان من عمليات تخريب قامت بها مجموعات من المستوطنين خلال حظر التجول .

٣ـ وافق وزراء خارجية دول المجموعة الاوروبية على رفع المساعدات لدول آسيا والشرق الاوسط على امتداد السنوات الخمس القادمة . وتنوي المجموعة الاوروبية من خلال اتفاقتي معونة زيادة معونتها لدول آسيا وامريكا اللاتينية الى ٢,٧٥ مليار وحدة نقد اوروبية اي ما يزيد بنسبة ٧٠ ٪ تقريبا عما قدمته

المجموعة من مساعدات الى هاتين المنطقتين في السنوات الخمس الماضية . وسوف تحصل بلدان جنوب وجنوب شرق آسيا على ٧٠ ٪ من مجموع هذه المساعدات . وتزداد معونات التنمية المقدمة من المجموعة الاوروبية الى الدول العربية الى ثلاث أمثال حجمها الحالي ، فقد وافق وزراء خارجية دول المجموعة على وجوب رفع ما يدفع الى الاردن ومصر ولبنان وتونس والمغرب والجزائر الى ٤٫٤ مليار وحدة نقد اوروبية .

٤ـ تصميم الأسلحة النووية الامريكية لا يتلاءم واشتراطات السلامة

اعلنت مجموعة من العلماء الامريكيين ان الأسلحة النووية الامريكية تحتاج في معظمها الى إعادة النظر في تصميمها وإدخال تعديلات عليها لمنع الأخطار التي قد تنتج عن تسرب مواد قاتلة منها او حدوث انفجار نووي. وقال التقرير ان غالبية الأسلحة النووية المستخدمة الآن في التَّرْسانة النووية الامريكية يجب ان تجرى عليها تعديلات لكي تتلاءم مع اشتراطات السلامة التي وضعتها الحكومة الامريكية .

HOMEWORK

*Tape

This lesson's broadcast consists of a complete news bulletin. Summarise in English. Make brief notes on any linguistic features that you think deserve comment.